LOST LANES

36 GLORIOUS BIKE RIDES
IN NORTHERN ENGLAND

JACK THURSTON

LOST LANES

CONTENTS

THE RIDES

MAP

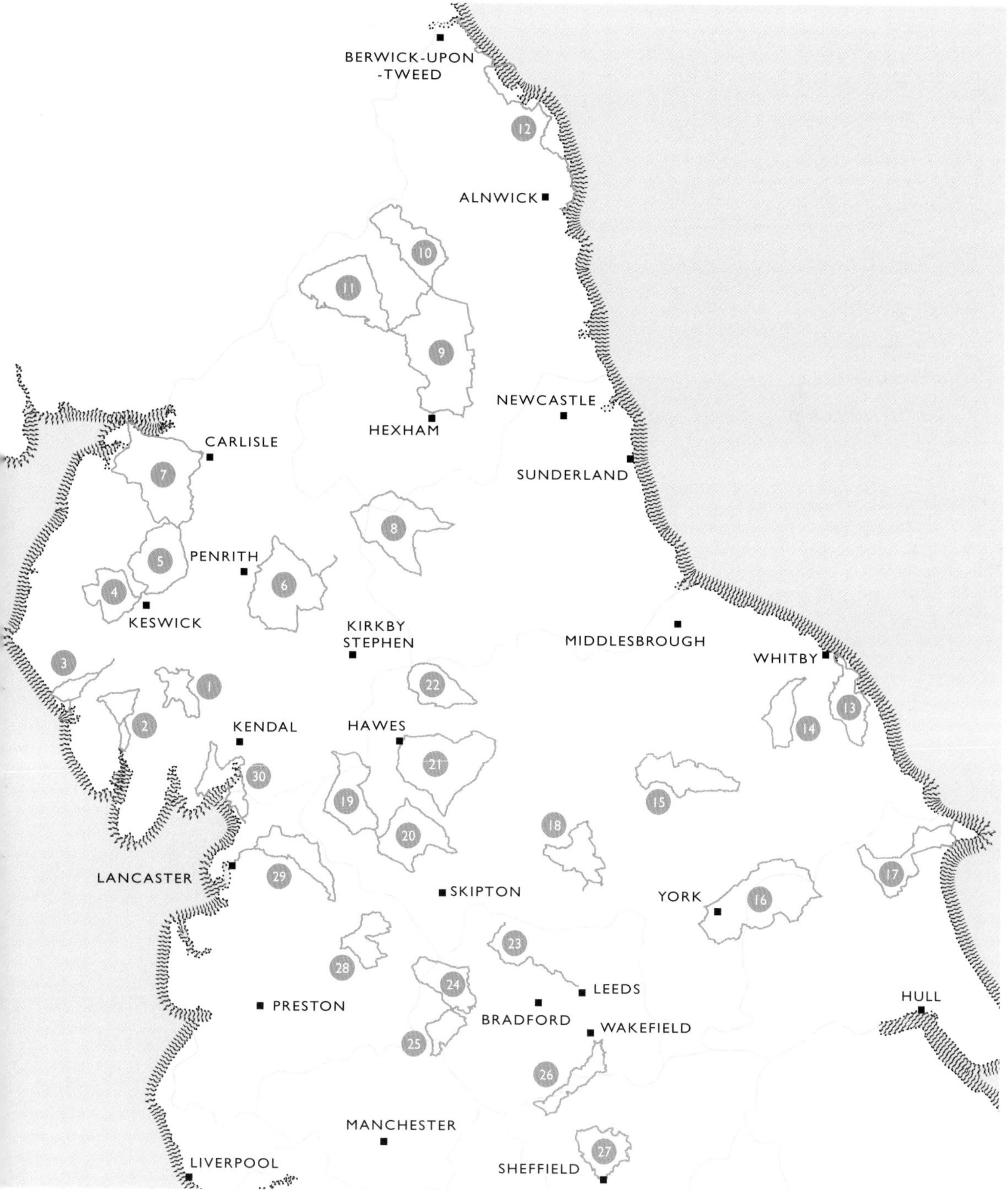

BERWICK-UPON
-TWEED
12
ALNWICK
10
11
9
NEWCASTLE
HEXHAM
CARLISLE
SUNDERLAND
7
8
5
PENRITH
6
4
KESWICK
KIRKBY
STEPHEN
MIDDLESBROUGH
WHITBY
3
1
22
13
14
2
KENDAL
HAWES
21
30
15
19
18
20
17
LANCASTER
29
SKIPTON
YORK
16
23
28
24
LEEDS
HULL
PRESTON
BRADFORD
WAKEFIELD
25
26
MANCHESTER
27
LIVERPOOL
SHEFFIELD

No.	NAME	COUNTY	START POINT	TRAIN STATION	GPX & DIRECTIONS
1	Poetry in Motion	Cumbria	Ambleside	Windermere (4km + ferry)	lostlanes.co.uk/01pm
2	Still Glides the Stream	Cumbria	Broughton	Foxfield (2km)	lostlanes.co.uk/02sg
3	Mountain High	Cumbria	Ravenglass	Ravenglass	lostlanes.co.uk/03mh
4	Liquid Landscape	Cumbria	Keswick	Penrith (33km)	lostlanes.co.uk/04ll
5	Back o' Skidda	Cumbria	Keswick	Penrith (22km)	lostlanes.co.uk/05bs
6	Garden of Eden	Cumbria	Appleby	Appleby	lostlanes.co.uk/06ge
7	Border Raid	Cumbria	Carlisle	Carlisle	lostlanes.co.uk/06br
8	The Roof of England	County Durham	Stanhope	Hexham (24km)	lostlanes.co.uk/08re
9	Over the Wall	Northumberland	Hexham	Hexham	lostlanes.co.uk/09ow
10	Northern Exposure	Northumberland	Elsdon	Morpeth (32km)	lostlanes.co.uk/10ex
11	Into the Wild	Northumberland	Bellingham	Haydon Bridge (25km)	lostlanes.co.uk/11tw
12	The Old North	Northumberland	Alnmouth	Alnmouth	lostlanes.co.uk/12on
13	Purple Haze	North Yorkshire	Whitby	Whitby	lostlanes.co.uk/13ph
14	Awheel in Wheeldale	North Yorkshire	Grosmont	Grosmont	lostlanes.co.uk/14aw
15	A Sentimental Journey	North Yorkshire	Thirsk	Thirsk	lostlanes.co.uk/15sj
16	The Way of the Wolds	East Yorkshire	York	York	lostlanes.co.uk/16ww
17	Hockney's Hinterland	East Yorkshire	Driffield	Driffield	lostlanes.co.uk/17hh
18	Song of Stone	North Yorkshire	Harrogate	Harrogate	lostlanes.co.uk/18ss
19	Three Peaks	North Yorkshire	Settle	Settle	lostlanes.co.uk/19tp
20	Up Hill Down Dale	North Yorkshire	Settle	Settle	lostlanes.co.uk/20ud
21	A Grand Day Out	North Yorkshire	Hawes	Ribblehead (on route)	lostlanes.co.uk/21gd
22	Secrets of Swaledale	North Yorkshire	Reeth	Kirkby Stephen (16km)	lostlanes.co.uk/22sw
23	A Very Yorkshire Journey	West Yorkshire	Leeds	Leeds	lostlanes.co.uk/23vy
24	Wuthering Heights	West Yorkshire	Hebden Bridge	Hebden Bridge	lostlanes.co.uk/24wh
25	A Calder Caper	West Yorkshire	Hebden Bridge	Hebden Bridge	lostlanes.co.uk/25cc
26	Hammer and Chisel	West Yorkshire	Wakefield	Wakefield	lostlanes.co.uk/26hc
27	Where there's Muck	South Yorkshire	Sheffield	Sheffield	lostlanes.co.uk/27mb
28	The Giant of Ribblesdale	Lancashire	Clitheroe	Clitheroe	lostlanes.co.uk/28gr
29	Take the High Road	Lancashire	Lancaster	Lancaster	lostlanes.co.uk/29hr
30	Brief Encounter	Lancashire	Carnforth	Carnforth	lostlanes.co.uk/30be

MILES	KM	ASCENT(m)	TERRAIN	GRADE
34	54	890	Mostly lanes, a few sections of good gravel track	Moderate
32	51	1063	Lanes and two short sections of A-road	Challenging
30	47	441	All lanes	Easy
35	55	972	Mostly lanes, optional sections of green lane and forest track	Moderate/Challenging
34	54	771	Lanes and one short section of railway trail	Easy
58	93	1491	Lanes, one short section of A-road	Moderate/Challenging
55	89	660	All lanes and tarmac cycleway	Moderate
49	78	1479	All lanes and quiet B-roads	Very challenging
65	103	1115	Mostly lanes, one short section of unsurfaced cycleway	Challenging
40	63	934	Lanes. Check military firing times.	Moderate
47	76	1054	Lanes and some extended sections of good gravel tracks	Challenging
57	92	550	Lanes and a few off-road sections which can be muddy when wet. Train return	Moderate
41	65	987	Mostly good forest tracks and unsurfaced railway trail, a few connecting lanes	Moderate
34	55	972	All lanes	Moderate
45	72	803	All lanes	Moderate
57	92	553	Mostly lanes and tarmac cycleway, one short off-road track	Moderate
54	86	530	All lanes	Moderate
42	68	663	Lanes and tarmac cycleway	Moderate
47	76	1073	All lanes	Challenging
39	63	968	Mostly lanes and one short section of rough stuff	Moderate/Challenging
48	78	1185	All lanes	Challenging
29	46	767	Road with an optional 3-mile section of track that's rough in places	Moderate
24	38	463	Mostly good canal towpath, some roads and one gravel track. Train return	Easy
34	55	1162	Mostly roads, 2 miles of off-road track	Challenging
24	38	471	Canal towpath, roads, lanes and short section of good gravel track	Easy
42	67	854	Mostly roads and lanes with a few sections of unsurfaced cycleway	Moderate
36	57	557	Canal towpath, roads, lanes and off-road tracks	Moderate
34	55	909	All lanes	Moderate
51	82	1276	Lanes, tarmac cycleway and one 5-mile section of gravel track	Challenging
43	69	816	Lanes, one short train link	Moderate

IN SEARCH OF

LOST LANES

—

Some people collect stamps, others collect coins, fine wines or cigars. I collect lanes.

The excitement starts when I open an Ordnance Survey map and begin tracing my fingers across its folds. I am looking for the thin yellow lines that might be good candidates for my collection. Before long, I'm lost in a daydream. In my reverie, all the lanes have a thick strip of grass up the middle and all the verges glitter with wildflowers. I am on my bike and bowling along past spring hedgerows laden with blossom and wooded glades carpeted with bluebells. Up ahead, a venerable oak tree overhangs the lane, sunbeams scatter through its leaves, and contented cows are quietly munching on a dew-spangled pasture.

None of this is shown on the map, of course. And while a good map has plenty of useful clues, it's all really just a way of whetting my appetite before I head out and explore them for myself.

My passion for lanes grew into a pastime and then into an obsession, which has led to writing books about them. This is the fourth. That you are reading this one is a clear sign that you, too, appreciate a good lost lane and probably share my view that the best way to explore the 'lanescapes' of the British countryside is by bicycle. Even so, it's never a bad thing to remind ourselves why this is true and, as we disappear for another day's riding, our friends and families can understand what it's all about or, even better, be persuaded to come along too.

Scientists who study these things have proven that – of every living thing and every machine yet invented – a human on a bicycle is the most energy-efficient form of travel. We humans are already pretty efficient when walking: better than a rabbit, a cow, a train or a helicopter (though not quite as efficient as a horse or a salmon). But a human on bicycle uses *one-fifth* of the energy of a person walking, and travels three times faster.

So, with that huge efficiency dividend, the question comes, how to spend it? The 'cycle-sport industrial complex', for which the media is a willing mouthpiece, urges us to use the efficiency of the bicycle always to go further and faster. Their ideal cyclist is one who racks up colossal distances and reaches the end of the ride utterly spent and craving the latest protein-enriched recovery drink. There is a place for extreme endeavours, but I prefer to use the efficiency of the bicycle in a different way. I seek to cover a distance that is big enough to give me the feeling of having gone somewhere, at a speed that's gentle enough to have been able to take it all in, and with a level of physical effort just a notch or two above 'taking it easy'.

Amazing though it is, efficiency is only one part of the appeal of the bicycle. As a means of travel, the bicycle is quiet and nimble, which makes it perfectly in tune with our dense network of narrow country lanes. On a bicycle you travel at the speed of the land. You don't just see and hear the world and the weather change around you, but you smell it and feel it. Physical effort heightens the senses and you feel everything with a greater clarity – the wind in your hair, the sun on your back, a drenching by rain or the chill of a crisp winter's day. You feel each incline in your legs, in your lungs, and the swooping descent in your stomach, the sway as you lean the bike this way and that to climb a hill or round a bend. The bicycle is a total immersion machine.

A bicycle makes travelling the lanes so easy. There is no hunt for a parking space. You can stop whenever and wherever you want. That could

be to admire the view, snap a photograph, look around an Iron Age hill fort or a poke about an abandoned mill, to have a bite to eat or make a brew, or to unfurl a sleeping bag and make a bed for the night. With a bicycle comes both a freedom and an inconspicuity that is frankly inconceivable in a car. A car is always a blot on the landscape, but a bicycle fits right in. The thrum of bicycle tyres and the tick and fizz of a freewheel are just as much a part of life in the lanes as the sound of the wind rustling in the tops of the trees.

Country lanes are not just a great way of finding peace and solitude, of getting closer to nature and discovering new places, they are portals for time travelling. Some lanes follow prehistoric trading routes, Roman military roads, pilgrims' ways, packhorse trails and old drove roads. Many more in number are the nameless,

ageless lanes which for centuries have seen nothing but the ordinary, everyday journeys that have gradually, over many generations, worn a line into the landscape.

The roads, tracks and byways of northern England offer almost unlimited possibilities; my intention is not to offer a comprehensive inventory of the lost lanes of the North but to showcase some of the best and to share my favourite way of exploring the country. Should the mood take you, I hope you will adapt and refine my routes according to your own interests and inclinations, and devise your own. As you pedal along, with map to hand, I hope you'll discover things that I may have missed and that, day by day, you'll amass your own treasured collection of lost lanes.

Jack Thurston, January 2020

MAPS AND NAVIGATION

MAPS AND ELEVATION PROFILES

The maps in the book are at a scale of just over 1:180,000. Therefore 1 cm on the map is about 1.8 km on the road and 1 inch on the map is about 3 miles. On the elevation profiles, 1 cm is about 150 metres of climbing and 1 inch is about 1,250 feet.

LEAVE THE BOOK AT HOME

This is a heavy book, and the last thing anyone would want to do is carry it around for a day's cycling. That's why all the information needed to ride the routes is available on the Lost Lanes website. As well as the maps in the book, there are Ordnance Survey maps, printable route sheets with turn-by-turn directions are available online. There are also GPX files for use with GPS navigation devices. The table on page 10 provides a website address for each ride where these resources can be found.

THE GENIUS OF THE NORTH

—

When writer Daniel Defoe toured the North in the 1720s, he warned his readers to steer clear of the Lake District. He described the area as "the wildest, most barren and frightful of any that I have passed over in England". He wrote that the hills possessed "a kind of inhospitable terror" and that the land "was no use or advantage either to man or beast". It wasn't only Defoe. Fear and loathing was the most common reaction to wild and unruly landscapes in those days. It was not without reason. The condition of roads ranged from terrible to non-existent, and travelling was painfully slow. What's more, the weather could be genuinely life-threatening, as Defoe discovered when he was caught in a snowstorm in the South Pennines, in August.

Today, instead of fearing wild places, we love them. A good share of the credit must go to William Wordsworth. In 1799, when still in their twenties, the young, Cumbrian-born poet and his sister Dorothy decided to make a small, damp cottage in the heart of the Lakes their home. This was no twee 'escape to the country' but an act of defiance, a wholehearted rejection of the fashionable, metropolitan way of life. It was a decision to embrace nature, in all its beauty and violent majesty, as muse and inspiration.

For the circle of poets and artists that gathered around them, a wild and untamed landscape was not an obstacle to be avoided or overcome, nor an opportunity for material exploitation, nor even a pleasing picture to look at, but something powerful and dynamic *to be experienced*. It meant getting outside and walking, sometimes for days at a time, overnight and across perilous terrain. Wordsworth is reckoned to have walked 175,000 miles in his lifetime (a mileage many cyclists would envy). His close friend Samuel Taylor Coleridge was the first person to walk all the biggest Lakeland fell tops in a single journey; he even coined the term 'mountaineering'.

Turning to nature was in part a reaction to a time of unprecedented political, economic and social upheaval at home and abroad. The French Revolution had overthrown an entire social order before turning sour with terror, dictatorship and war. Meanwhile, the industrial revolution was forging a new and, at times nightmarish, world.

It was in the North that coal, iron, engines and railways first combined to unleash a new economy and a new kind of society. Weaving, for centuries a cottage industry in the Pennines, grew to the point where Lancashire's mills were producing one-third of the world's cotton goods and employing more than half a million people. Factory work was better than farm work, and industrial towns and cities swelled with migrants from the countryside. Mill owners made huge fortunes and bestowed northern cities with the most impressive civic buildings of the Victorian era. But poverty, squalor and disease were endemic. In towns and cities, the air was thick with smog; rivers were rank with effluent of every kind.

One small blessing for the people who endured long days of monotonous and often dangerous work was the beautiful and comparatively unspoilt countryside almost within touching distance. Most factory workers were not long removed from the fields and retained an affinity for country ways. Many cultivated a detailed knowledge of the natural world. And yet, at the very same moment, wealthy landowners were fencing in the countryside for grouse shooting and pursuing new, more efficient methods of farming. The rambling clubs and footpath preservation societies that sprang up in opposition to these changes across the industrial north during the 1820s marked the first beginnings of popular movements for outdoor leisure and access to the land.

Caldbeck Fells

It is a rich irony that Wordsworth, whose politics were once radical and democratic, and who did more than anyone to promote the Lakes as a destination, actively campaigned against the coming of the railways. He feared an influx of day-trippers from the Lancashire mills would spoil its rural character. John Ruskin, another famous champion of the Lakes, echoed Wordsworth in decrying the railways. He also took aim at cycling, which he saw as the latest manifestation of a dangerous new cult of speed. But the genie was out of the bottle, and the bicycle soon found a ready market in northern towns and cities.

As a practical tool for personal liberation, cycling went hand in hand with the continuing clamour for political, social and economic reform. The Clarion Cycling Clubs of the North combined a quaint, homespun English form of socialism with a love of fellowship and the outdoor life. Channelling the Romantic poets, a member of the Rochdale Clarion wrote in 1896, "Closeness to nature leads to nearness to man, to an intimate pervasive consciousness of human fraternity". The movement grew big enough to establish a network of Clarion clubhouses, of which just one still remains, near Nelson in Lancashire.

The radical ramblers and socialist cyclists of the early twentieth century were just the latest manifestation of northern radicalism with a strong link to the landscape: the preacher George Fox was moved to found Quakerism after experiencing a vision of great multitudes from the summit of Pendle Hill; John Wesley made horseback journeys to preach his humane, stripped-down Christianity in the open air; and Chartists and their supporters, banned from meeting in towns, flocked to the moors in their tens of thousands to hold 'monster meetings' to call for universal political rights. By the 1880s, campaigners were using mass trespass as a tactic to push for the right to ramble, and outdoors enthusiasts from the North played leading roles in the establishment of the National Trust and the Youth Hostels Association, and the creation of national parks.

ALL POINTS NORTH

When the weather conditions are just right (or wrong, if you're a shepherd gathering in your flock or a cyclist with a few miles still to ride), a fearful wind blows down the steep western slope of the North Pennines. This powerful north-easterly is known as the Helm Wind. It is the only named wind in the British Isles, taking a place alongside celebrated winds like the Mistral, the Sirocco and the Chinooks. The wind is accompanied by a heavy bank of cloud just above the Pennine crest and, a few miles west, a long cigar-shaped mass of rolling cloud known as the Helm Bar. I can't say if the Helm Wind is England's windiest wind but, if it weren't special, why would anyone bother to give it a name? The genius of northern landscapes is more than their physical power and scale. It is their potency as a muse for creative minds, a stage set that can intensify the most compelling human dramas and a canvas for the expression of thoughts, feelings and ideas.

As the highest point in the Pennines, Cross Fell is as good as anywhere to contemplate the geography of the north (though perhaps not when the Helm Wind is blowing). The Pennines is the backbone of northern England, a chain of moors and minor mountains running from the Peak District to the Tyne Gap. It is at once a unifying spine and a physical barrier dividing the wetter and warmer counties of the west from the drier and colder counties of the east. At its simplest, the geology of the Pennines is a thick layer of porous limestone overlaid by a layer of coarse millstone grit, all raised up by a mass of hot granite deep underground. Movement of the earth's crust has caused everything to crack and fold, while glaciers and rivers have sculpted hills and valleys, and carved crags and gorges. On either side of the Pennines are England's richest coalfields, the compressed remains of dense forests and swamps that contain within them the preserved sunlight of tens of millions of tropical summers.

Cross Fell stands in 175 square miles of moorland through which no road passes. By my reckoning it is the largest block of wild country in England. The only buildings are the radar station on Great Dun Fell, a mountain bothy and a handful of shooting huts, sheepfolds and abandoned lead mines. To the east is a vast expanse of blanket bog from where the mighty rivers of the Tyne, the Wear and the Tees begin their journeys to the North Sea. To the west the peaks of the Lake District are clearly visible, though they have an entirely different geology to the Pennines. The dark slates and craggy volcanic rocks are among the oldest rocks in England. Their precipitous slopes, jagged profiles and proximity to the coast make them seem much higher than they really are. Long, sparkling fingers of water only add to the unique atmosphere of a mountain country in miniature; Lakeland's cols and passes are tough cycling challenges.

North of the Lakes are the lowlands of the Solway Plain and the border with Scotland. Legally agreed in 1237, it is one of the world's oldest land borders. A thousand years earlier, the Romans had built a defensive wall from the Solway Firth along the northern slopes of the Tyne valley all the way to Newcastle. Beyond the wall lies the Northumberland interior. The wooded expanses of the Kielder Forest and the rounded Cheviot Hills are the most sparsely populated part of England. These once violent borderlands shade imperceptibly into Scotland's southern uplands.

From Berwick-upon-Tweed to Newcastle, the Northumberland coast is the most pristine coastline in the North. Mile after mile of dune-fringed sandy beaches, shimmering mudflats and salt marshes are interspersed with sturdy little harbours and medieval castles in varying states of ruin.

South of here, from Newcastle to Middlesbrough, is the once-mighty industrial heartland of the north-east. The area was built on coal, iron and steel, shipbuilding, heavy engineering and the manufacture of chemicals, armaments, glass, plastics and more. Many iconic industries have gone but the death of the industrial north has been greatly exaggerated, as anyone who has cycled past Teesside's refinery skyline will affirm. Further south rise the iron-rich Cleveland Hills, now part of the North York Moors National Park. The northernmost outcrop of a band of Jurassic rock that stretches all the way to Dorset on the south coast, it's a moorland plateau cut by deep, lush ravines and broad, glaciated dales with a coastline of cliffs and picture-postcard fishing villages built up implausibly steep lanes.

Lake District

Yorkshire Dales

The Cross Fell range

Yorkshire Wolds

Still today, right across the North, moors are managed primarily for grouse shooting. And it all revolves around a single plant: *Calluna vulgaris*, a purple-flowering heather. Grouse like to eat the young and tender heather shoots and to build nests in bigger and older heather bushes. Gamekeepers burn strips of heather in rotation to maintain a habitat to maximise grouse numbers. Without the burning and grazing by sheep, the moors might well revert to a more natural mosaic of woodland, scrub, bog and open habitat. This, advocates argue, would help reduce flood risk, soak up atmospheric carbon emissions and provide for a more diverse range of wildlife. On the other hand, what's good for the grouse is also good for other ground-nesting birds like curlew and golden plover, as well as for lizards, short-eared owls and honey bees, whose hives are placed up among the flowering heather over the summer. The debate about the future of grouse moors will run and run.

On the south-west edge of the North York Moors are the Hambleton and Howardian Hills, a crescent of buttery Jurassic limestone that could easily be mistaken for the Cotswolds. South of here, across the River Derwent, are the Yorkshire Wolds, England's most northerly expanse of chalk downland. They terminate in white cliffs higher than the famous ones in Dover. This is more grist

to the mill for those Yorkshire folk who believe their county is a smaller version of England, only better. It's hard to argue with them. Yorkshire has all the ingredients – landscape, economy, history and people – to stand alone as a proud and contented small European country. If Croatia can do it…

One issue that would immediately confront the leaders of the newly independent nation-state is that Yorkshire is shrinking. The coastline south of Bridlington is disappearing faster than any coastline in Europe, thanks to rising sea levels caused by climate change. Already Yorkshire's Mississippi, the Humber is expected to widen dramatically. In in a new delta landscape, Hull will become Yorkshire's New Orleans, a prospect that would have delighted Philip Larkin, the city's celebrated poet and jazz buff.

Inland is York, the Roman capital of the North (or Central Britain as the Romans knew it). One of Europe's finest medieval cities, it sits in the wide fertile plains of the Vale of York, with the equally agricultural Vale of Mowbray to the north. West of York, all the way to the foothills of the Yorkshire Dales, is a swathe of prosperous market towns and well-to-do villages and farms. The southern half is the 'golden triangle', the well-heeled hinterland of Leeds, another once-mighty industrial city that is the modern – though still unofficial – capital of Yorkshire.

Between Leeds and Sheffield is the rolling countryside of towns and villages where life once revolved around the South Yorkshire coalfield. For an industry that didn't just drive the economy but provided jobs – and meaning – to entire communities, coal mining was swept away with ruthless speed in the 1980s. Today, above ground at least, almost nothing remains but memories. Winding gear has long since been dismantled and sold for scrap, spoil heaps flattened and planted with greenery. Mines have been replaced by retail parks, warehouses and distribution centres where, as the Barnsley poet Ian McMillan puts it, "the ceilings are higher and the work is hard in a very different way".

Manchester is the biggest city in the North and part of an emerging megalopolis that extends all the way to Liverpool. Things are a lot better now than they were in the 1930s when the Yorkshire writer and broadcaster J. B. Priestley visited and wrote, "between Manchester and Bolton the ugliness is so complete that it's almost exhilarating. It challenges you to live there." The mines, the furnaces and the chimneys belching black smoke are now gone. So too are the slag heaps that once smouldered like volcanoes, and the slums of back-to-back housing have either been cleared or renovated.

There is still plenty of industry – and grit and grime – but outside of town centres, residential suburbs and the remaining pockets of agriculture, large parts of West Lancashire's coastal plain is neither recognisably urban, suburban nor rural. It is an 'edgeland', to use the term first coined by writer and campaigner Marion Shoard. A fascination with these new mosaics of abandoned, overgrown and chaotic 'non-places' dotted by retail parks, business centres, industrial estates and gravel pits is brilliantly conveyed by Paul Farley and Michael Symmons Roberts in their book *Edgelands: Journeys into England's True Wilderness*. They observe that "cars are a defining characteristic of the edgelands". Getting around by bike isn't easy.

By contrast, the canals and packhorse trails and moorland roads to the north of Manchester are perfect for exploring by bicycle. Here are the open moors that were blank pages for the imagination of Emily Brontë, deep cut by valleys of glistening moss, gnarled roots and glowering rocks. What's more, several mill towns have emerged from slow economic decline with an influx of creative people with countercultural leanings and, with flourishing music and arts scenes, are great places to live.

Further north are the Yorkshire Dales and its less-visited neighbour the Forest of Bowland. Each one is a paradise for cyclists, whether on quiet lanes through pretty stone-built villages or on remote byways and off-road tracks. The southern edges of the Dales are the most visited, and things get steadily wilder the further north you go, all the way to Tan Hill, north of Swaledale. Here is the highest pub in Britain, complete with resident snowploughs; it marks the transition from the Dales to the North Pennines, with Cross Fell just a few miles further north.

RIDE THE SEASONS

"To everything there is a season", say the scripture and the folk song. And it's true the further north you go, with much more pronounced changes in the season, from snowdrifts in the Pennines to drenching Atlantic storms in the north-west and howling Siberian gales in the north-east. Winter is deeper and longer in the north; spring comes as much as a month later than in southern climes. But when it does come, it happens faster and feels like an even more powerful bursting forth of new life.

Spring is sweet wherever you are, but it doesn't get much sweeter than in the Bowland Fells and the Ribble Valley and in the Hambleton Hills and the remote dales on the southern edge of the North York Moors, with Farndale renowned for its displays of wild daffodils. Each flower of the early spring gets its own week or two in the sun from snowdrops and crocuses through to primroses, wood anemones to bluebells, violets and cowslips, with blackthorn the first of the hedgerow plants to wake from winter, its tiny pinky-white flowers appearing before its leaves. The soundtrack to spring in the Bowland Fells is the chatter of wading birds such as lapwing, curlew, snipe and redshank. There are powerful smells too, most of all the wild garlic that carpets moist shady woodlands.

David Hockney spent several years in the lanes and fields of the Yorkshire Wolds, painting the changing landscape through the seasons. He pinpointed a time in late May as 'Action Week', the moment on the cusp of late spring when the hawthorn bursts into great billowy clouds of blossom and the roadside verges are at their most colourful. Then, all of a sudden, the bright, zesty shades of springtime darken to the duller greens of summer. Ecologists might bemoan the agricultural intensification of the Wolds but can't deny that the yellow fields of oilseed rape, some well over a hundred acres, are an arresting sight. Despite all the agrichemicals, drifts of crimson poppies still appear all the way through summer. From mid-April to mid-June botanists flock to upper Teesdale to see rare alpine plants including the intense blue spring gentian which thrives in the calcium-rich grassland. May and June are the best months to spot puffins and other seabirds nesting in the cliffs around Bempton in East Yorkshire and further north on the rocky headlands of Northumberland's heritage coast.

In midsummer the days are longer the further north you go. In Northumberland the effect is really noticeable, with just a couple of hours between twilight and the first light of dawn. Coastal wildflowers come into their own in the dunes, meadows and salt marshes. Upland hay meadows are a rare sight these days, but they can still be found in the upper reaches of Langstrothdale, Swaledale and Dentdale in the Yorkshire Dales and in upper Coquetdale in Northumberland. Mid- to late July is haymaking time, and meadows are at their peak for a month before the meadows are cut. High summer is also the best time to take the plunge in the many waterfalls and swimming holes of the Yorkshire Dales.

Wherever you stand on the rights and wrongs of grouse shooting, the mile upon mile of purple heather on the grouse moors, the North York Moors, the Bowland Fells, the Yorkshire Dales and the South Pennines are a magnificent sight. August is the best time to see them, though the colours can linger well into September. The grouse shooting season starts on the 'Glorious' 12th of August.

The Lake District is a wonder at any time of year, and somehow the fells manage to absorb huge numbers of visitors and rarely feel overcrowded. August is by far the busiest month and narrow Lakeland roads can become choked by motor traffic. If you're exploring by bicycle, this is the month to go somewhere else. It is far better to wait until October when the colours change to yellow, orange and deep gold, the skies are clear blue (if you're lucky) and spectacular cloud inversions fill the valleys with mist. There's also a much better choice of accommodation in the Lakes if you visit off-season.

By November, winter will have taken the North into its icy grip. With shorter days and grey skies the norm, a bright winter's day out on the bike is a genuine morale booster. If you wrap up warm and take care if the roads are icy, there's a whole winter world to enjoy. Trees look utterly different in their naked silhouettes, the low sun casts long shadows and a hard frost causes the land to sparkle. If it snows, it's always a fun challenge to head uphill once the snowploughs have cleared the way. On winter days it's worth planning a stop or two en route for a chance to defrost from behind the steamed-up windows of a cycling-friendly café or beside the blazing log fire of a pub.

The night sky in winter is clearer than in summer, and across Northumberland, the North Pennines, the Yorkshire Dales and the North York Moors there is a winter season of stargazing events open to the public with astronomers and telescopes on hand. And you can always just head out on your own on a clear night around the time of the new moon when the sky is at its darkest. You will see even more with a pair of binoculars.

NORTHERN SOUL

While three of the boundaries of the North are self-evident (the Irish Sea, the North Sea and the Scottish border), the southern border is a source of great debate. It's all a matter of where you're looking from. To a Cockney born to the sound of Bow Bells, the land of cloth caps and whippets begins a few miles past Barnet. For a Geordie, anywhere south of Sunderland doesn't count as the real North.

A popular candidate is the Watford Gap in Northamptonshire. As well as marking a geological divide, it sits on an important north-south linguistic boundary. To the north of the line people tend to pronounce the words *bath*, *laugh*, *grass* and *chance* with a short a sound (as in *cap*) while to the south they say

North York Moors

them with a long a sound (as in *hard*). Geography professor Danny Dorling proposes another line based on life expectancy, poverty, education and skills, employment, and wealth. His line is a wiggly diagonal running from Grimsby to Gloucester, putting the Forest of Dean in the North and Lincoln in the South. Not only that, the line may be steadily moving southwards, as the North swallows up ever more of the Midlands. And this is where both these divisions fall down: they overlook the existence of the Midlands as a place of its own.

For this book I have chosen the ancient line from the Humber to the Mersey via Sheffield as my southern limit of the North. I have omitted the Peak District entirely if only to leave some hill country for the next *Lost Lanes* and not to spread the rides even more thinly. The Humber-Mersey line goes back to the days after the Romans left Britain. Germanic settlers turned the land that would one day become England into seven Anglo-Saxon mini-kingdoms. There was a clear dividing line between the Kingdom of Northumbria (the people *north* of the *Humber*) and the Kingdom of Mercia (the people of the border with Wales). The line was reinforced by

the invasion of Vikings from Denmark who settled in Northumbria and made their capital in York. Many northern place names are Norse in origin, as are northern landscape words like *fell*, *dale*, *beck* and *foss*.

Even after the unification of England, with its strong Nordic influence, the North remained a place apart. Soon after the Norman conquest, the elites of the North, aided by their Viking allies, rebelled against England's new rulers. In response, William the Conqueror subjected the North to a merciless campaign of colonial suppression. Tens of thousands of people were slain or died from starvation. Many more were made refugees in their own lands. Ever since, being ruled from 'that London' has rarely pleased the North nor benefitted its people, most of all through the long, hard years of deindustrialisation.

And here is the reason why debates over the North-South divide are so forcefully argued. The idea of the North is not just about geography but about character and identity. Writing in the 1930s in *The Road to Wigan Pier*, George Orwell describes "a curious cult of Northernness" based around a belief that the "the northerner has grit, he is grim, dour, plucky, warm-hearted and democratic". By contrast, the people of the South are "snobbish, effeminate, and lazy", and Southern England is "one enormous Brighton inhabited by lounge-lizards". It's an enduring caricature. Maybe because there's a kernel of truth in it. The six northern writers nominated for the 2020 Portico Prize, which celebrates literature that best evokes the spirit of the North, were asked what it means for them. Among the qualities mentioned were resilience, black humour, a rebel streak, friendliness to outsiders, absurdism and "a joy in spite of everything". But also stubbornness, bloody-mindedness, suspicion of change, sentimentality and nostalgia.

Time and again, the North has been a breath of fresh air, whether in the literal sense on its moors and mountains, or culturally and metaphorically in fresh ideas and new ways of doing things. The radio broadcaster Stuart Maconie who hails from Wigan and has written whole books about northernness, argues that the northern state of mind boils down to "embracing that life is short and work is hard and that London is not the answer to everything". Who could argue with that?

PRACTICALITIES

___

ROUTES AND MAPS

The rides in this book range from 25 to 65 miles but most are around the 35- to 50-mile mark, which for most people is a good distance for a leisurely day's ride, or a half-day ride for the energetic. I've deliberately refrained from adding timing to the rides, as it's better to ride at one's own pace than somebody else's. However, based on a typical touring pace of 10 to 12 miles per hour, allowing for hills, most rides require 4 to 6 hours in the saddle. If, like me, your idea of a good day out on the bike includes taking time to stop for a pub lunch or a cream tea (or both!), a river dip and an afternoon nap, then ending the day by scrambling up a hill to watch the sunset, you may want to split the longer rides over a couple of days. To this end, I've recommended good places to spend the night, along with the listings of recommended pubs, cafés and bike shops. A night in a historic coaching inn or a boutique B&B is lovely, but some of my best bike overnights were spent out in the open, tucked up in a bivvy bag looking up at the Milky Way.

Much of the North is hilly, upland country. Wherever possible I've tried to go around hills rather than over them, but the road often does go up. This will have an impact on the time it takes to ride a certain distance and the basic level of fitness required for some of the hillier rides. I've indicated the total vertical ascent of each ride, which should give a clue as to how hilly it is; the elevation profiles may also help. If the hills get too much, there's absolutely no shame in walking. In the very early days of the Tour de France, most riders – including the winners of the race – pushed their bikes up the biggest mountains.

The maps in the book are best used in combination with a good paper map, such as the Ordnance Survey's 1:50,000 Landranger series. The cost of buying them does add up, but they can be borrowed from most public libraries or viewed and printed online from Bing.com/maps or Gpxeditor.co.uk. The Ordnance Survey's own smartphone app and third-party apps like ViewRanger are viable alternatives to paper Landranger maps.

As well as the maps in the book, there is a printable route sheet and a GPS navigation file for each ride on the Lost Lanes website (*lostlanes.co.uk*). Each ride has its own web page and these are listed in the table on page 10.

GPS NAVIGATION

GPS navigation is less good for exploring and improvising than a paper map, but it excels when following a pre-planned route, assuming the batteries don't run out. Cycling-oriented GPS units will alert you if you make a wrong turn and, as well as a little map, the more modern models will give you an elevation profile so you know where the hills are coming up. For each ride in the book (except the organised group rides) the web page above includes a GPX file for use in a GPS navigation device or smartphone. For plotting new routes for GPS navigation, I recommend *ridewithgps.com*, *bikehike.co.uk* and *gpxeditor.co.uk*, as all include a full selection of map sources and satellite imagery, and have simple, intuitive interfaces. Garmin has long been the market leader in cycling GPS devices but I've had a very good experience with a Wahoo ELEMNT device while researching this book. Smartphones also provide GPS navigation and the Ride with GPS app is a good one to try. Download base maps to your phone so that you're not relying on a data connection while riding. I tend to switch my phone to Airplane mode to conserve battery. It is always worth carrying spare batteries and/or a charging pack.

Forest of Bowland

TAKE THE TRAIN

I have tried to make the rides accessible by train but rail service in the North is by no means comprehensive. Two Together railcards offer big savings, as do Small Group tickets for groups of three or more. Breaking a return journey is a good way to get more value from a single fare, and most rail companies allow unlimited breaking on the return leg of an open return journey, including overnight breaks, so long as the ticket is still valid (they are usually valid for one month). For a week away, a Rover ticket may be a good option. Trains tend to have between two and six dedicated bicycle spaces, and booking in advance is the best way to secure a stress-free journey and avoid disappointment. Most inter-city services now require cycle reservations, though these can sometimes be done up to 15 minutes before travelling or via a smartphone app. Some train companies restrict access to trains during peak commuting times when most trains are at their busiest. If the train already has its full complement of bikes or, if you've not made a reservation, a pleading look and heartfelt gratitude can work wonders. Most train conductors are human.

ANY KIND OF BIKE

The rides in this book can be ridden on any bike that's in good mechanical order and the right size for the rider. Low gearing makes climbing hills much less daunting. A triple chainring or a sub-compact double and/or at least a 34-tooth rear sprocket can tame the steepest gradient. Tyre choice makes a huge difference to the sensation of riding a bike. Good-quality tyres between 28mm and 40mm in width are a sensible all-round choice for a fast and comfortable ride. Avoid really knobbly tyres as they slow you down on surfaced roads. A touring bike is an ideal choice: the Dawes Galaxy has always been a good place to start, but a new breed of gravel and adventure bikes are perfect if you're travelling light and want more of a road bike feel. These light bikes have the feel of a road bike but with disc brakes that perform well in all weathers, nice wide tyres and all the fittings for racks and mudguards if required.

Average temperatures are lower and rainfall higher in the North of England – with the most rainfall west of the Pennines. Check the forecast at the Met Office website (or the smartphone app) and be prepared to ride accordingly. It's no fun pushing on through a monsoon; better to take cover until the storm passes, as they usually do. Unless it's the middle of a heatwave, I consider mudguards an essential item: it's bad enough being rained on from above; it's worse to have a jet of mucky water sprayed up from below.

LIGHTS, LOCKS AND LUGGAGE

When riding in the dark, a set of lights is a legal requirement. Good lights are well worth the money and modern battery-powered LED lights are nothing short of amazing. On dark country lanes, supplementing lights with reflective material is a good idea. A power bank is also handy if your phone, lights or GPS device needs topping up. Dynamo lighting is making a revival, and there are special adaptors to use the power from a hub dynamo to recharge a power bank. In the countryside, a lock is often unnecessary but can be a good precaution, especially if you plan to leave your bicycle unattended for any length of time. A small cable is enough to deter an opportunist, but in cities or large towns where professional bike thieves may be lurking, it makes sense to pack a heavier, more secure lock. If riding with a group, a single lock can secure several bikes.

Money, a basic tool kit, a snack and a mobile phone can be stuffed into a very small rucksack, bumbag or in the rear pockets of a cycling jersey. Anything heavier is more comfortable if carried on the bicycle itself, in either a handlebar bag, a saddlebag or a pannier.

CLOTHING AND SHOES

In spite of the images of Lycra-clad racers presented in magazines and on television, the overwhelming majority of people in the world who ride bikes do so in ordinary clothing. Of course, there's nothing wrong with indulging a taste for the latest cycling gear and donning a cycling uniform of one kind or another, but the reality is that whatever clothing is comfortable for a walk in the park will be fine for riding a bike in the countryside for a few hours.

Tight jeans with raised seams can be uncomfortable on longer rides. Padded shorts or underwear provide extra comfort if needed. In heavy rain, thick cotton and denim gets waterlogged, won't keep you warm, and takes longer to dry than wool and synthetic, technical fibres.

Riding in the rain isn't much fun but lightweight, waterproof fabrics are a big improvement over old-style plastic pac-a-macs. For night rides and camping trips, a few extra layers are a good idea, as well as a warm hat. From autumn to spring, windproof gloves keep fingers nice and warm. I am a fan of the outdoor clothing companies Páramo and Patagonia. Both make outstanding gear and put ethics and environmental responsibility at the heart of their businesses.

Cycling-specific shoes are unnecessary for all but the most race-oriented cyclists. The way I see it, large, flat pedals with good grip mean I can wear almost any type of shoe. But if you like the feeling of 'clipping in' I'm not going to argue.

WHEN THINGS GO WRONG

Compared to running a car, the cost of maintaining a bicycle, even if all the work is done by a professional bike mechanic, is minuscule. Assuming the bicycle is in generally good mechanical order, the skills and tools necessary to mend a puncture and fix a dropped chain are enough to guarantee self-sufficiency on day rides. A truly worst-case scenario means phoning for a taxi to the nearest train station.

A basic on-the-road repair kit consists of the following:
- Tyre levers, a pump and a couple of spare inner tubes
- A puncture repair kit
- Screwdrivers and hex keys required for removing wheels, adjusting brakes and tightening racks, mudguard fittings and the seat-post clamp
- A few cable ties (zip ties) can come in handy, and a bungee cord is useful for securing bikes on trains.

Learning a little about how a bike works not only saves money but comes with a warm, satisfying glow of self-sufficiency. Some tasks are best left to a professional, but the basics are easily mastered. If there's nobody around to give a hands-on lesson, buy a bike maintenance book or look online for instructional videos, such as those by Patrick Field at *madegood.org*.

RIDING SAFE AND SOUND

Riding a safe distance (at least 1.5m/5ft) from the roadside and at least a car door's width from any parked cars is much safer than hugging the kerb. Making eye contact with other road users helps everyone get along.

On roads, it is cyclists who suffer most from the boorish attitude that 'might makes right', and we should be at pains to preserve the civility of traffic-free paths shared with walkers, skaters and horse riders. Be aware that other people are out enjoying themselves, too, and may not be paying full attention. Approach horse riders with caution and a verbal greeting to let the beast know that you're human.

When leading group rides with slower or less experienced cyclists, rather than speed off and leave the group trailing in your wake, aim to ride at a pace that's no faster than the slowest riders can comfortably manage.

CLUBS AND ORGANISATIONS

Membership of Cycling UK (CUK), British Cycling or your local cycling campaign group not only helps these worthy organisations campaign on behalf of cyclists but also brings benefits like discounts in bike shops, member magazines, third-party insurance and free legal advice in the very unlikely event of an accident. Most local cycling groups have programmes of free or very nearly free rides, which are a great way of discovering new places and meeting new people, with an experienced ride leader taking care of all the navigation and planning tea and lunch stops.

There are also good online communities of cyclists. The CUK web forum brims with expert touring and technical advice. Yet Another Cycling Forum leans towards audax and touring and the Bear Bones Forum is good for bikepacking. All are lively places to look for advice, to find out about rides, routes and events, and even to find riding companions.

The National Trust and English Heritage maintain hundreds of amazing properties across the country, but entry fees can be high if you're just making a fleeting visit while out for a day's bike ride. If you're the kind of person who enjoys visiting historic buildings and sumptuous gardens, an annual membership makes sense and all funds help contribute to the upkeep of their properties. Similarly, the RSPB, the Wildlife Trusts and Plantlife are member-funded charities that do important work conserving and restoring the natural environment and maintain some superb nature reserves.

Finally, another way to immerse yourself in all things bicycle is to listen to The Bike Show, the long-running cycling podcast that I present (*thebikeshow.net*).

BEST FOR

WILD CAMPING

—

Many of the routes in this book could be used as the basis for a short overnight trip with a bivvy bag or lightweight tent. These are best on a long summer evening when there's plenty of time to ride for a few hours, and find a remote and beautiful spot to enjoy a simple camp dinner before settling down to a night under the stars, safe in the knowledge that you'll be returning to 'civilisation' the next day. There's no need for all the stressful preparation and packing for a longer trip. If you forget something, it's no big deal. The worst that can happen is a bad night's sleep.

Rather than bother cooking an elaborate camp dinner, for a one-nighter I tend to fill a Thermos flask with something hot and hearty, and perhaps boil water for couscous and a hot drink on a lightweight camping stove; packing a loaf of bread means the stove can be left behind altogether. Perhaps the biggest challenge on an overnight trip is carrying enough water, though in the uplands you can usually find a clean stream (pack a portable water filter or sterilisation tablets if you want to be doubly safe). Two large bike bottles per person allows for drinking plenty while riding, some for cooking in the evening and enough for tea or coffee in the morning. If you do run dry, most pubs will be happy to refill your bottles. Or just knock at a door.

There's nothing more relaxing than sitting out under the night sky, well-fed and chatting with friends, feeling the cool night breeze with no more disturbance than an owl hooting in the woods and sheep bleating in the valley below. The cares of real life are left far behind. Then again, maybe this is the real-life and it's the office that's the illusion?

DO IT YOURSELF

One of the great things about Northern England is that you're never too far from the uplands, and a little preparation is helpful in identifying a good wild camping spot. Look at the Ordnance Survey's 1:25,000 (Explorer) maps together with satellite imagery to get an idea of the terrain (they're both available free online at *bing.com/maps*). Google Street View is handy for checking out the lie of the land, and *geograph.org.uk* is a useful source of images along tracks and bridleways. The best spots are on open ground or in woods, well out of sight of any dwellings, preferably with access from a bridleway or footpath rather than a road. Even on day rides, I'm always keeping an eye out for the perfect camping spot for a future overnight trip.

In lowland areas it's prudent to camp a little way away from any houses or buildings and out of sight of early morning dog walkers. A tent adds weight and can make you more conspicuous, but it gives a sense of security and more protection from the elements and midges, which can be bad in northern summers. Sleeping in a hammock or under a tarp is an alternative to a tent or a bivvy bag. It all comes down to a matter of taste: some find hammocks uncomfortable, others dislike the confinement of a tent.

Though wild camping is broadly legal in Scotland, this is not yet the case in England. However, in the Lake District, there is a long tradition of upland wild camping and the National Park gives the following guidelines: camp above the highest fell wall, and well away from towns and villages; leave no trace; just one or two tents; stay for one night only. Elsewhere, it's at your own risk. Asking for the landowner's permission isn't always easy as there's rarely an

indication of who owns the land. It's easier to ask for forgiveness afterwards than to seek permission in advance. I take the pragmatic view that if I'm unseen and leave no trace, the landowner is unlikely ever to know, or to care, that I've spent the night. If there's a No Camping sign, think twice. Arrive late and leave early. Be sure not to disturb any livestock or trample crops or sensitive habitats like bluebell woods, and definitely don't light a fire without permission. Best of all, leave the land in a better state than you found it by collecting any litter left by other visitors. Most landowners are more concerned about long-term squatters or car-campers leaving disposable barbecues and other trash than people travelling light on their bikes.

The following rides in this book are particularly well suited for adapting into a wild camping trip.

No. 2 STILL GLIDES THE STREAM

The Western Fells are the highest part of the Lake District and the least visited. There are good wild camping options with spectacular sunset views above the Roman fort at Hardknott and on the track which leads north from beneath the fort up the River Esk. On lonely Birker Fell, a good track leads to Devoke Water, from where you can look out across the lake to the Irish Sea and, if you can bear the cold, take a morning dip.

No. 5 BACK O' SKIDDA

Wild camping has a long tradition in the Lakes and any of the Lakeland rides could work well as overnight trips. The Caldbeck Fells are a little-visited area with some good access tracks that are perfect for finding a secluded wild camping spot. Another option is Skiddaw House, an off-grid, car-free hostel in the heart of the massif – the best cycling access is from Threlkeld or Bassenthwaite. Booking is essential.

No. 12 THE OLD NORTH

A coastal wild camp is a rare pleasure and the Northumberland coast is the most remote stretch of coastline in England, with huge sandy beaches fringed by dunes and lots of open land and salt marsh. Driftwood campfires are frowned upon these days, as they destroy the habitat of the rare beachcomber beetle *Nebria complanata*. What's more, treated timber often found on beaches can release toxic smoke.

No. 15 A SENTIMENTAL JOURNEY

Near the end of this route is the craggy, steep-sided edge of the Hambleton Hills. An old drove road runs along the ridge, which now forms part of the Cleveland Way long-distance walking and cycling path. The path follows the very edge all the way to Roulston Scar, where there are the remains of an Iron Age hill fort and England's largest and most northerly hillside white horse. The views from the edge are famously good and, with a western aspect, it's a perfect place to watch the sunset. Sutton Bank and Gormire Lake are popular beauty spots, so wild camping requires discretion (it's safest to head north away from the crowds). There's a great campsite option at the aptly named High Paradise Farm just north of Boltby Bank.

Dent's House, Wensleydale

No. 21 A GRAND DAY OUT

If you prefer a roof over your head there are a couple of unofficial bothies in Wensleydale. They are actually grouse-shooting lodges owned by the Bolton Estate, but they are usually left open to be used by passers-by as shelters. Dent's House is above Castle Bolton, and best accessed via the track from the road across Grinton Moor. The Greenhaw Hut is above Carperby. It's prudent to pack a shelter of your own just in case they're in use or locked. Both huts have wood stoves and it's best to bring your own fuel. Always observe the bothy code by leaving shelters cleaner and tidier than you found them.

No. 22 SECRETS OF SWALEDALE

Upper Swaledale is a farmed landscape but there are plenty of places where a discreet wild camper could find a place to stop for the night, especially if you follow the rough stuff option on this route via Crackpot Hall. There are options either down by the river or further up the hillside among the old mine workings. Likewise, on exposed moors beyond the Tan Hill Inn, there are good tracks leading off in either direction – it can get cold and windy at night at this altitude, even in high summer.

No. 29 TAKE THE HIGH ROAD

With a long section of rough stuff across the grouse moors of the Forest of Bowland, this ride is a perfect overnight adventure, though depending on your timing, you might choose to do the route in reverse, and camp out on the way back towards Wray. In the summer months, be sure to keep fairly close to the track so as not to disturb any ground-nesting birds. The best place to unfurl a bivvy bag or pitch a tarp is in the grassy areas around a shooting hut, abandoned farmstead or sheepfold.

LONG WEEKENDS

———

All the rides in this book can be done in a single day but they are easily adaptable into weekends away or multi-day mini-tours, either by splitting a ride over two days or by linking two or more rides into a longer tour.

There has never been more choice in places to stay: from tiny campsites where you can get back to nature, through camping barns and youth hostels, all the way to grand coaching inns, plush B&Bs and boutique hotels. I have put some of my own recommendations in each ride's listing of pubs and pit stops. These are my suggestions for multi-day tours linking two or more rides.

SOUTHERN AND WESTERN LAKES [RIDES No. 1, 2 & 3]

These three rides are easily linked into a 110-mile tour that takes in the grand scenery in the heart of the Lakes and the more dramatic and less-visited western fells. There is train access from Windermere and a lake crossing by ferry from Bowness. The tour could be enlarged to the south with the addition of Ride No. 30, which starts at Carnforth railway station with a linking section on lanes from Bowland Bridge via Winster to the Bowness ferry.

The Lake District has more youth hostels than anywhere else in Britain, often in grand Victorian Lakeland houses.

NORTHERN LAKES [RIDES No. 4, 5 & 7]

This 125-mile tour starts at the West Coast Main Line at Carlisle and heads for Keswick, the capital of the northern lakes, where it makes two loops, one around the Skiddaw Massif and the other past Derwent Water, Buttermere, Crummock Water, Loweswater and Bassenthwaite Lake. There are some great overnight options, from the cosy Kirkstile Inn to the isolated, off-grid Skiddaw House (accessible on off-road tracks from the Skiddaw Loop).

NORTHUMBERLAND INTERIOR [RIDES No. 9, 10 & 11]

This 150-mile tour of the wildest reaches of the Northumberland interior begins in the Tyne Valley at Hexham or Corbridge, or you could ride over from Newcastle on the scenic and mostly traffic-free route beside the river (NCR 72). Ride No. 9 gets you to Bellingham, a village that makes a perfect base for exploring the Kielder Forest, Coquetdale and the Otterburn Ranges.

Old Chamber, Hebden Bridge

YORKSHIRE WOLDS [RIDES No. 16 & 17]

Taken together, with a connecting route from Huggate to Driffield on NCR 164, these two rides are a 140-mile tour from the medieval city of York to the coast at Bempton Cliffs and Bridlington and back. The tour takes in many of the highlights of the Yorkshire Wolds like the dry river valleys of Water Dale and Millington Dale, the lost lane of Woldgate and the giant standing stone in Rudston, and there is an easy detour to the remains of Wharram Percy. Along the way it passes a good handful of the scenes David Hockney painted while he was living in Bridlington.

YORKSHIRE DALES [RIDES No. 19, 20, 21 & 22]

The Yorkshire Dales is a brilliant place to explore by bike. There are plenty of quiet lanes and some top-notch rough stuff too. These four routes can be combined into a 180-mile tour that takes in the full range of landscape types: the Dales, from the dramatic limestone in and around Malham, the gritstone table mountains of the Three Peaks, the bleak, high moors of Tan Hill and mile upon mile of the broad glacial valleys that are the signature of the Dales.

SOUTH PENNINES AND THE FOREST OF BOWLAND [RIDES No. 24, 28 & 29]

These three rides can be linked together as a 145-mile 'Tour of the Roses' from the Upper Calder Valley in West Yorkshire via Pendle Hill to the Forest of Bowland in Lancashire. A couple of linking sections are required, the first from Trawden to Barley (7 miles, initially on NCR 68) and from Bolton-by-Bowland to Slaidburn (5 miles on NCR 90).

Rydal Water

WILD SWIMMING

———

It is scientifically proven that you can revive tired leg muscles by submerging them in cold water. I've used this trick any number of times and it really works. A wild swim is not only good for the body, but good for the mind. The late Roger Deakin, ecologist, nature writer, campaigner and wild swimmer, coined a new word – endolphins – for the thrillingly pleasurable, all-encompassing rush of a wild swim.

In his seminal book *Waterlog*, Deakin compiles a whole new watery vocabulary to describe the simple, timeless activity of immersing yourself in a natural body of water, be it a river, a lake, a stream or the sea. He uncovered obscure, rarely used words associated with wild water – dook, loom, winterburna, bumbel – and described the feeling of water itself, from a languid, meandering river to a furiously frothing mountain stream.

Perhaps Deakin's greatest contribution is debunking the view that swimming in nature is a dangerous, daredevil pursuit. It can be, if you ignore common sense, but many more people drown in their own baths each year, and we don't plaster bathrooms with warning signs and barbed wire.

Northern England is blessed with countless lakes, tarns, rivers and waterfalls that are perfect for a plunge. Make sure you're not trespassing on

private land, be alert to the strength of the river's flow and check the depth and temperature before jumping in. Very cold water can be a dangerous shock to the unprepared. In the sea, check that there are no dangerous tides or currents.

No. 1 POETRY IN MOTION

This ride is as rich in great swim spots as it is in big Lakeland vistas. The peaty waters of Blea Tarn are good but what makes it is the location beneath the almost Alpine crags of the Langdale Pikes. Coniston Water has good, easily accessible shingle beaches at its northern end.

No. 4 LIQUID LANDSCAPE

Quiet, comely Buttermere and its bigger, wilder neighbour Crummock Water are both well located for a pre-lunch dip on this ride. Take a picnic to enjoy on the waterside or ride on for a pub lunch at the Kirkstile Inn.

No. 10 NORTHERN EXPOSURE

The Upper Coquet Valley once flowed freely with illicit moonshine but today it is a river swimming paradise. There are too many places to list them individually, but some of the best are in the few miles upstream of Alwinton. For a hot summer's day only, as the water is freezing.

No. 12 THE OLD NORTH

The Northumberland coast has tremendous wild swimming, though the chill waters of the North Sea are always bracing. This ride hugs the coast and there's plenty of choice, from the long sandy beaches of Embleton Bay and Bamburgh Castle Sands, to little-known places like Coves Haven on Holy Island and Sugar Sands south of Craster.

Dunstanburgh Castle

River Wharfe near Grassington

No. 20 UP HILL DOWN DALE

The limestone landscape of the Yorkshire Dales makes it a wild swimming paradise. This ride passes Janet's Foss waterfall, which has a swimmable plunge pool, the beach and falls on the River Wharfe near Grassington and, near the end of the ride, Stainforth Force, a perfect spot to revive tired legs.

No.21 A GRAND DAY OUT

The first half of this ride is a festival of climbing, and the combination of Fleet Moss and Park Rash will leave your legs in need of a reviving swim. Fortunately there is a series of good swim spots in the River Ure in the last miles of the route: Aysgarth Falls is justly popular with locals and summer crowds, while nearby Redmire Falls is the hidden secret.

No. 22 SECRETS OF SWALEDALE

At the top end of Swaledale the village of Keld is surrounded by waterfalls and great swim spots. No wonder, Keld comes from the Old Norse word *kelda*, meaning a well or a spring. Wain Wath waterfall is popular and has a grassy bank for relaxing, while Kisdon Force, a little downstream, is for the adrenaline junkies, with two waterfalls and big, terrifying cliff jumps.

Janet's Foss

Coquetdale

BEST FOR

FAMILIES

———

For new cyclists and younger children, sharing even quiet country lanes with motor traffic can be unnerving. Fortunately, thanks to the dogged work of Sustrans, enlightened local councils and national parks, there are miles of traffic-free cycling to enjoy. Riverside paths, off-road cycle tracks and bridleways are an enjoyable, safe and confidence-building alternative to roads and lanes. Canal towpaths are a legacy of the Industrial Revolution now repurposed as leisurely cycling and walking routes. Likewise, a handful of the many northern branch railways that fell victim to Dr Beeching's axe now enjoy a second life as traffic-free cycling and walking paths.

Most of the rides in this book are too long and too hilly for very young children or absolute beginners, but several of the rides have family-friendly sections that are perfect as stand-alone rides for younger and less experienced cyclists, and for people whose mileage is limited.

Northumberland coast

No. 1 POETRY IN MOTION

This ride has several sections on traffic-free trails, each of which would make for a good destination for a ride with kids who are not yet confident on the roads or strong enough for hills. Ambleside to Grasmere is pure Wordsworth country, with the views you'd expect. Little Langdale to High Tilberthwaite is short but with lots to see, from Cathedral Quarry to Andy Goldsworthy's sheepfold. The traffic-free cycle path on the west shore of Windermere between the Bowness ferry north and super, child-friendly Wray Castle is perfect for families.

No. 11 INTO THE WILD

The lakeside trail around Kielder Water is perfect for younger riders, though, at 26 miles round and constantly undulating, most will find it a challenge to complete. On certain days from March to October (currently Wednesdays and Saturdays) the Osprey ferry plies the southern end of the lake and is a way of shortening a ride or providing a bailout if required. There are only four sailings a day so be sure to check the timetable.

No. 12 THE OLD NORTH

Much of this route is traffic-free, flat and by the sea. In other words, perfect for kids. The best sections are between Boulmer and Embleton, which mixes off-road tracks with quiet lanes, and from the Holy Island causeway north to Berwick-upon-Tweed, where the coastline is a bit wilder.

No. 13 PURPLE HAZE

As a largely traffic-free route, this is a good one for children. The coastal Cinder Track from Whitby to Scarborough is intensely scenic, though the surface is rough in places. Older children who

Rochdale Canal

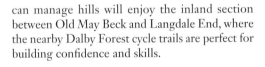

River Lune Cycleway

can manage hills will enjoy the inland section between Old May Beck and Langdale End, where the nearby Dalby Forest cycle trails are perfect for building confidence and skills.

No. 18 SONG OF STONE

The Nidd Valley Greenway from just west of the pretty estate village of Ripley to the spectacular small market town of Knaresborough (with a side spur to Harrogate) is a lovely bit of traffic-free cycle infrastructure that makes use of old railway lines. Local campaigners defeated plans to use the route for a new 'relief road' and their hard work has secured this precious green corridor along the steep-sided Nidd Gorge for the enjoyment of future generations.

No. 23 A VERY YORKSHIRE JOURNEY

The first section of this ride from Leeds to Saltaire is a perfect day out for kids or new cyclists. The canal towpath is flat and well surfaced and there's lots to see along the way and Salt's Mill is a perfect destination. The railway runs along the valley which offers a handy return or bailout. The canal continues all the way to Liverpool, though the towpath surface gets rougher west of Keighley.

No. 25 A CALDER CAPER

The Rochdale Canal runs for 32 miles between Sowerby Bridge and Manchester. It makes light work of crossing the Pennines and connects through the Upper Calder Valley. This ride includes the most scenic section between Hebden Bridge, Todmorden and Littleborough, crossing the Pennine watershed. It's traffic-free, but south of Todmorden it gets rough under wheel so is more suited to older children. The gravel routes around the reservoirs at Blackstone Edge are great for kids and learners.

No. 29 TAKE THE HIGH ROAD

Lancaster is blessed with some great traffic-free cycling routes. The first section of this route from Lancaster to Caton is alongside the River Lune (NCR 69) and a perfect route for children and new cyclists. The scenery is lovely, especially the famous viewpoint at Crock O' Lune. Another great traffic-free circuit is on the old railway line to Morecambe (NCR 69) where you can ride north along the seafront to Hest Bank and pick up the canal towpath (which goes all the way to Carnforth) for the return back to Lancaster.

PUBS

The pub, the church and the green are three focal points that help define the quintessential English village. Yet across the country, pubs are closing at an alarming rate. Many of those that remain have become quasi-restaurants offering upmarket dining or, at the other end of the scale, rural sports bars with giant television screens and Saturday night karaoke.

But the pub is fighting back. Pub food is more varied than ever, more pubs have rooms for overnight stays, and micro-breweries are breathing new life into the art of beer-making. As well as crusading for traditional brewing, the Campaign for Real Ale (CAMRA) maintains a useful online directory of historic pub interiors.

Northern England has some brilliant breweries, too many to list here. At the Jolly Fisherman in Craster (Ride No. 12) a friend and I drank pints of Workie Ticket from the Mordue Brewery that came as close to a spiritual experience as it's possible to have in a pub. Here are a few other favourites to look out for. Pale ales: Pennine Pale (Allendale Brewery), White Rat (Rat Brewery, Huddersfield), Loweswater Gold (Cumbrian Legendary Ales, Hawkshead). Amber bitters: Landlord and Boltmaker (both Timothy Taylor, Keighley), Pendle Witches Brew (Moorhouses, Burnley). Darker brews: Old Moor Porter (Acorn Brewery, Barnsley), Old Tom (Robinsons, Stockport), Dark Mild (Bank Top Brewery, Bolton).

Northern England is also home to the miraculous institution that is the railway buffet bar. Stalybridge and Bridlington (Ride No. 16) are well-preserved originals, while those at Sheffield, York, Carnforth, Whitby and Dewsbury are loving restorations.

No. 2 STILL GLIDES THE STREAM

The Wordsworths stopped in at the Newfield Inn in Seathwaite and would probably recognise the cosy free house in a 16th-century whitewashed stone cottage if they went back there today. Eskdale has a wealth of pubs and three of them – the Woolpack Inn, the Brook House Inn and the Boot Inn – hold a beer festival every June. For many, the utterly unspoilt Blacksmiths Arms in Broughton Mills is the best pub in the Lakes.

No. 4 LIQUID LANDSCAPE

By a long way Britain's most visited national park, the Lake District has more than its fair share of tourist traps. With a huge guaranteed footfall, landlords here have less incentive to do things right. The Kirkstile Inn is an exception and is a really good country pub. Real ales, hearty food, log fires, flagstones, timber beams and a great location on quiet Loweswater. Further on, near Bassenthwaite Lake is the Pheasant Inn, a Georgian coaching house little changed in generations.

The Kirkstile Inn, Loweswater

The Fat Cat, Sheffield

The Newfield Inn, Seathwaite

No. 22 SECRETS OF SWALEDALE

The Tan Hill Inn is the highest pub in the British Isles, at 528m above sea level. There are snow-ploughs stationed outside, and in January 2010 New Year's Eve revellers were stuck inside for three days and night by heavy snow – the ultimate pub lock-in. It's a touch touristy but on a wild and windy day on the moors it's a welcome sight. Down the hill in the former lead mining village of Langthwaite is the tiny Red Lion serving good beer, pasties and pork pies.

No. 25 A CALDER CAPER

Don't tell Hebden Bridge, but Todmorden has the best pubs in the Upper Calder Valley. The Golden Lion takes prime position on the canal quayside and puts on live bands and occasional DJ sets by the likes of Jarvis Cocker, Andrew Weatherall and Andy Votel. Thai food with a good selection of local beers. Also worth a stop are the Bare Arts Brewery and micropubs The Alehouse and The Pub. In Cragg Vale nose-to-tail chef Fergus Henderson's protégé Rob Owen Brown serves up local seasonal food at very reasonable prices at the Hinchliffe Arms. Back in Hebden Bridge, Calan's micropub and The Old Gate are good places to relax after a ride. Unless you're on a Ted Hughes / Sylvia Plath pilgrimage in which case you'll want to make tracks to Stubbing Wharf, no longer a "gummy dark bar".

No. 26 HAMMER AND CHISEL

Perfectly located at the very end of this ride is the Kings Arms on Heath common, just upstream on the riverside path from Wakefield. The village itself consists entirely of buildings dating from the 15th to 19th centuries and the pub is a Grade II listed building. Inside it's a warren of cosy rooms and snugs lit entirely by gas lights.

No. 27 WHERE THERE'S MUCK

Sheffield is a city of fantastic pubs and some of the best are in Neepsend and Kelham Island at the end of this ride. The community-owned Gardeners Rest and the Fat Cat are traditional boozers with a friendly vibe. The Riverside is a more modern affair, with good, hearty food served all day and a terrace overlooking the River Don. In Rotherham the Cutlers' Arms is worth a short detour if you're a fan of ornate Edwardian interiors – wood panelling, glazed tiles, terrazzo floors and Art Nouveau stained glass. The rambling George & Dragon in Wentworth has outlasted the Earls Fitzwilliam in the big house, and there's plenty of memorabilia on the walls. In Oughtibridge the Travellers Rest is run by Samuel Smith's brewery with its winning formula of a historic interior and good, cheap beer.

GOURMETS

In his defence of English cooking, George Orwell singles out a trio of indisputably Northern delicacies: Yorkshire pudding, Wensleydale cheese and kippers. To that we might add Lancashire hotpot, sticky toffee pudding, pan haggerty, Henderson's Relish, Eccles cake and parkin, the spicy ginger cake that's claimed by both Lancashire and Yorkshire. The truth is that every area of Britain has its own specialities and there is much less of a north-south divide in English food than there is an east-west divide, owing to the differences in climate and rainfall, and therefore crops and livestock, on each side of the Pennines.

Orwell argued that English food had a poor reputation because the best of it could only be found in the home and never in restaurants. He was writing in 1945 and so much has changed since then. In the 1970s the concept of the gastronomic country house hotel was born on the shores of Windermere in the Lake District, and this may well have sparked England's fine dining scene. Pubs were once for drinking beer, and pub food went no further than a pork pie or a pickled egg. Now food is as important as booze to the economic viability of the pub. Add to that the welcome resurgence of farmers' markets and local and artisan food producers, from bakers to brewers to picklers and cheesemakers.

Whereas motorists have to stop at petrol stations to refill their tanks, cyclists have to stop to fill their bellies, and there's never been more choice. For more on the local and regional specialities see Dorothy Hartley's classic *Food in England*, and *The Taste of Britain* by Laura Mason and Catherine Brown. For where to find it, *Eating England* by Hattie Ellis has a useful directory of suppliers.

No. 12 THE OLD NORTH

Kippers have been smoked in Robson's smokehouse in Craster since 1856. First split and brined, the herrings are then suspended over smouldering wood fires for 16 hours. The result is a delicacy that is exported far and wide but perhaps best enjoyed within wafting distance of the 20ft-high brick chimney that's just up from the compact harbour. The smell is unmistakable. Thick, buttery, fishy and resinous. First, it sets up shop in your nostrils and then, once you've eaten one, it will stay with you for the rest of the day. For the crème de la crème of the kipper world, they are amazingly inexpensive, and as well as served hot in Craster's café and pub, they are sold vacuum-packed for later.

Robson's Smokehouse, Craster

Whitby

Little Salkeld Watermill

No. 13 PURPLE HAZE

It's a matter of north-south debate where fish-and-chips was first served. There are competing claims from Lancashire and the East End of London, both dating the idea to the 1860s. However, fried battered fish and fried potatoes are certainly much older. The alchemy came when they were served together, wrapped in paper, sprinkled with salt and liberally doused with malt vinegar, and eaten outside as steam rises in clouds. Whatever their origins, in my view there's a far better chance of finding good fish and chips up north than down south. And the very best odds are down by the harbour in Whitby. There are at least half a dozen world-class chippies, but Trenchers is the current top dog, winner of a National Fish and Chip Award in 2019.

No. 15 A SENTIMENTAL JOURNEY

As you'd expect in the well-heeled, chocolate box villages of Yorkshire's miniature Cotswolds, there are some top-notch country dining pubs in the Hambleton Hills. Two of Yorkshire's five Michelin-starred restaurants are within a few miles of each other at Oldstead (Tommy Banks's Black Swan) and Harome (Andrew Pern's Star Inn). They are both very upmarket, with dazzling tasting menus, though the Star Inn also offers a fixed menu three-course lunch for £25. More gastropub than fine dining is the excellent Stapylton Arms in Wass, while Helmsley Walled Garden has a good café in its Victorian glasshouse serving produce from the kitchen garden.

No. 21 A GRAND DAY OUT

Wallace and Gromit may have saved Wensleydale cheese. Sales were flagging in the 1990s and the future of the creamery in Hawes was uncertain. The popularity of the animated clay characters, and Wallace's penchant for the pale, crumbly Yorkshire cheese, revived the brand. The creamery is thriving and offers tours of the cheesemaking process. My favourite is the tangy farmhouse version named in honour of Kit Calvert, a local cheesemaker who saved the cheese once before, by keeping the old ways going during the 1930s. This ride also passes the White Lion in Cray, an old drovers' pub with a reputation for serving some of the best food in the Dales.

No. 30 BRIEF ENCOUNTER

On the southern edge of Lakeland, the village of Cartmel is a foodie mecca. The old smithy is home to L'Enclume, regularly voted the best restaurant in Britain, with prices to match. Rogan & Co is its more affordable offshoot. There's also the Pig and Whistle pub and the Cartmel Village Shop, whose sticky toffee puddings are well on the way to world domination. In Unsworth's Yard there are artisan food shops selling all the ingredients for a picnic worthy of a Michelin star. Further on, the Mason's Arms on Cartmel Fell's Strawberry Bank is a superb 16th-century inn serving hearty and delicious food.

HISTORY

——

History is all around us, and so much more than what is in the history books. But you need to slow down to take it in, which makes the bicycle the perfect vehicle for time-travelling. The history of the North goes right back to the retreat of the glaciers at the end of the last ice age. Relics are all around: from prehistoric stone circles, medieval castles and Elizabethan country mansions, to the mills, mines, railways and canals that made the North the global hub of the Industrial Revolution. Waves of invasion and migration have shaped the North – the Roman Wall, Celtic crosses, Anglo-Saxon villages, Viking tombs, Norman castles, French monasteries and Scandinavian field barns. And it's not just bricks and mortar. The North even has its own language of the landscape: a medley of native Brittonic, Old English, Norse and Norman. The movement of people and ideas has not let up: it's what defines the rich tapestry of the North of today.

No. 6 GARDEN OF EDEN

The North has been the home of the wealthiest aristocratic families in Britain. None were richer or more ostentatious than the Earl of Lonsdale at

Brougham Castle

the turn of the 20th century. Known as the Yellow Earl, he was described as 'almost an Emperor, not quite a gentleman' and brought his estate to the brink of bankruptcy. Lowther Castle is now Cumbria's top visitor attraction with a network of cycle tracks through its parkland. This ride also passes Bronze Age henge monuments, Brougham castle and Roman fort, a working watermill and the ruins of Shap Abbey.

No. 7 BORDER RAID

The border town of Carlisle is rich in history – from its time as a Roman and Norman garrison to its boom years as a textile mill town. This route follows the Roman wall along the Solway, passing a trio of small, fortified churches where people took refuge when under attack by lawless border clans known as 'reivers'.

No. 8 ROOF OF ENGLAND

The North Pennines has a history of lead mining that goes back to Roman times. Industrial archaeology is all around on this ride. There are preserved mining and metal workings at Allenheads and Nenthead. A heritage steam railway (bikes welcome aboard) connects Stanhope with the main line at Bishop Auckland. A few miles off-route is the major lead mining museum at Killhope.

No. 12 THE OLD NORTH

This ride passes the coastal castles of Dunstanburgh and Bamburgh, the latter having a history going way back to the Celtic people of 'the old north' who spoke a language similar to Welsh. It also takes in the Holy Island of Lindisfarne, an early centre of Christianity in Britain.

Fountains Abbey

Bingley Five Rise Locks

No. 15 A SENTIMENTAL JOURNEY

Starting at the market town of Thirsk, this ride passes a series of honey-stoned villages, the grand medieval abbeys at Byland and Rievaulx, the remains of Helmsley Castle, a stately Georgian pile at Nunnington, and Shandy Hall, where Laurence Sterne wrote his groundbreaking novel *Tristram Shandy*. Near the end, the route crosses Hambleton Road, one of the best-preserved drove roads in the North.

No. 18 SONG OF STONE

There is more fine architecture in this ride starting from Harrogate, an elegant Victorian and Edwardian spa town with recently restored Turkish Baths. Ripon's Gothic cathedral has a 7th-century Saxon crypt and there is a trio of town museums in the old workhouse, courthouse and prison. Nearby Fountains Abbey is a magnificent ruin that speaks to the power and wealth of the medieval monasteries, while Ripley is an attractive estate village beside a 14th-century country house.

No. 23 A VERY YORKSHIRE JOURNEY

There's some landmark industrial history on this ride along the Leeds and Liverpool Canal, from the Leeds Industrial Museum to Salt's Mill and Saltaire (built as a model town for mid-19th

century workers), and Five-Rise Locks in Bingley. The climax of the ride is a crossing of Ilkley Moor, with or baht 'at.

No. 27 WHERE THERE'S MUCK

There's more industrial history on this ride from the steel city of Sheffield. The ride passes through the Wentworth Estate built by the Fitzwilliam family. Their vast landholdings included swathes of the South Yorkshire Coalfield. The collieries are gone but the Elsecar Heritage Centre has some old headgear, a steam railway and a working Newcomen beam engine, while Wortley Top Forge is an iron forge dating back to 1640 that's now an open-air museum.

No. 28 THE GIANT OF RIBBLESDALE

Almost untouched by the modern world, the village of Downham is one of the loveliest villages in England. It lies on the slopes of Pendle Hill, a hill with more history than most, from the sad and macabre Lancashire witch trials to the exultant vision that came to George Fox, the founder of Quakerism. There's strong radical history here, too. The Clarion House near Barley is the last remaining of dozens of clubhouses established by local socialist societies; it's still going strong.

BEST FOR

ARTS AND CULTURE

As the writer Christopher Morley put it, "The bicycle, the bicycle surely, should always be the vehicle of novelists and poets." Artists and musicians, too, drew inspiration from the bike, from French cubists and Italian futurists in the early 20th century to Ai Weiwei's huge installation Forever Bicycles, David Byrne's *Bicycle Diaries* and Kraftwerk's Tour de France records. All of the following rides include a cultural destination, from an art gallery to a house or garden created with artistic vision, or a landscape with strong literary connections.

No. 1 POETRY IN MOTION

The Lake District was the first place where landscape and culture became truly intertwined. This ride starts in the realm of the Lake Poets and passes close to Dove Cottage, where William and Dorothy Wordsworth made their first home and hosted a stream of fellow Romantics. The route passes an Andy Goldsworthy sheepfold on the way to Coniston Water, where John Ruskin chose to spend his last decades. Coniston's museum is now home to Ruskin's archive. Beatrix Potter lived, wrote, drew and kept sheep in and around Hawkshead. Her home at Near Sawrey and a Beatrix Potter gallery at Hawkshead are owned by the National Trust and open to the public.

No. 11 INTO THE WILD

The 26-mile-long lakeside trail around Kielder Water has more than a dozen world-class public art installations by artists, makers and architects. There are giant rotating wooden chairs, a forest head you can climb into, and a stone wave chamber that gives a new way of experiencing the light and sounds of the massive reservoir. At the top of the long climb to Blakehope Nick is a pentagonal timber shelter designed by students at Newcastle University's School of Architecture.

No. 17 HOCKNEY'S HINTERLAND

After decades in California, when David Hockney came home to Yorkshire, it was to rediscover the lanes and byways of the Yorkshire Wolds, the places he had first encountered as a schoolboy on a bike. It was the perfect subject, constantly changing with the seasons and the rhythms of the farm year. This ride (and Ride No. 16) take in a handful of Hockney locations including Woldgate, an ancient road that's now a very lost lane.

No. 23 A VERY YORKSHIRE JOURNEY

There's more Hockney on show at Salt's Mill in Saltaire, the factory town built by local industrialist Titus Salt that's become a UNESCO World Heritage site. Once the biggest mill in Europe, Salt's Mill is now an arts space with a constantly changing programme of events and exhibitions, as well as the biggest single collection of Hockneys.

No. 24 WUTHERING HEIGHTS

The landscapes of the Upper Calder Valley are an elemental force in the writings of the authors and poets who were born here, lived here or moved here. Ted Hughes was born in Mytholmroyd where Scout Rock "provided both the curtain and back-drop to existence". Emily Brontë lived and died over the hill in Haworth and wandered wild and free on the moors, which provide the setting for *Wuthering Heights*. Benjamin Myers, a shining star of today's literary scene, is powerfully engaged with the topography, mythology, poetry and the people of the Upper Calder Valley.

Brontë Parsonage Museum, Haworth

Touchstone Fold, Tilberthwaite

The Nick, Kielder Forest

No. 26 HAMMER AND CHISEL

The coal mines have gone but this West Yorkshire / South Yorkshire area is becoming a cultural magnet. This ride starts at the Hepworth Gallery in Wakefield and passes through the Yorkshire Sculpture Park, a 500-acre 'gallery without walls', both world-class art galleries. Further on, Cannon Hall has a fine collection of ceramics, and the Cawthorne Victoria Jubilee Museum is the sole survivor of John Ruskin's dream of a national network of small village museums.

Lakeside Trail, Kielder Water

UPS AND DOWNS

—

Freewheeling downhill is a sensation that's hard to describe but impossible to forget. It's akin to being a bird in flight: a lightness of being, a rush of speed and a feeling of carefree excitement that just makes you want to smile. But there is a catch: what goes down must also go up. Riding a bicycle uphill is, at the very least, an acquired taste. On the flat, the bicycle multiplies a modest effort into effortless speed. On a climb, the tables are turned. Suddenly the miracle machine is a dead weight to carry.

Yet there are times when climbing, the combination of effort and concentration, approaches a state of grace. Every rhythm, from beating heart to heaving lungs to pumping legs and spinning pedals, comes together in a symphony of ascent. That's why it's so addictive and why people write entire books and websites about the best cycling climbs. At other times, the best thing to do when faced with a really steep climb is to get off and walk. And there is no shame in that. In fact, it gives you all the more time to soak in your surroundings. The North is home to England's steepest, longest and hardest cycling climbs and some of its most pleasurable descents.

No. 2 STILL GLIDES THE STREAM

Hardknott Pass is a beast among Lakeland climbs. Fortunately this ride takes the somewhat easier side from Cockley Beck. Even so, its initial tight hairpin ramps are up to 30%. The tarmac has a hard time sticking to the mountain, and only the strongest cyclists and those with ultra-low gears can keep the pedals turning, let alone stay in the saddle. This route can be paired with Ride No. 1 for a five-star feast of climbing: the connecting road is Wrynose Pass, Hardknott's slightly less evil twin.

No. 6 GARDEN OF EDEN

For Simon Warren, Britain's leading connoisseur of cycling climbs, Great Dun Fell "has no peers, there is no comparison". The tarmac surface is good but it's not a public highway, rather a service road up to the air traffic control radar station on the second-highest peak in the Pennines. The top half of the road is closed to motor vehicles but open to cyclists. In total the climb is 4½ miles long at an average gradient of 9%, rising to a maximum of 20%. The view from the top is immense. It can be windy and cold, even in summer, so pack some gloves and a jacket for the descent.

No. 8 ROOF OF ENGLAND

When you find yourself cycling between snow poles and riding past a ski resort you know you're up high. The North Pennines have the highest and most exposed roads in England. During the winter they can be snowbound for days or weeks on end, hence the skiing. Even in summer, when valleys like

Yad Moss

Hardknott Pass

Great Dun Fell

Langstrothdale

Teesdale are studded with rare wildflowers, there are none of the crowds that flock to the Lakes and the Dales. It's a place where you can find blissful solitude.

No. 14 AWHEEL IN WHEELDALE

The North York Moors is made up of ridges and dales with about 200 vertical metres between the two. The roads often go straight up, no long hairpins to reduce the gradients around here. This ride passes the foot of Chimney Bank in Rosedale, and shares the title of steepest road in England with Hardknott Pass in Cumbria. Though not part of the route, it's a test for any cyclists, though beware, as its nickname is 'chain breaker'. This ride dodges the big hills and, almost magically, it is a ride of more memorable descents than lung-busting climbs.

No. 21 A GRAND DAY OUT

When the Tour de France came to Yorkshire in 2014 the county went cycling-mad. An estimated 2.5 million people lined the roadsides over the two days of racing. Many were disappointed, however, that the Tour's organisers wigged out of taking the race over the country's toughest climbs. Perhaps the two toughest climbs in the Yorkshire Dales are Fleet Moss and Park Rash. This route takes in both of them, and they are difficult in different ways: Fleet Moss is long but fairly gradual – a test of attrition. Park Rash is half the length but it makes up for it in steepness: nasty, brutish but not as short as you hope. The reward for each climb is a long, swooping Dales descent that repays every ounce of effort on the climb, with interest.

ROUGH STUFF

Gravel bikes and adventure bikes are the hottest trends in the bike industry, and a sign that more and more people want a bike that's capable of handling unsurfaced byways and tracks but can zip along at a good lick. But off-road cycling goes back a long way. In the very earliest days of cycling, most roads were pretty rough, and even as they were surfaced with tarmac many cyclists still loved seeking out old byways and tracks.

Some of the earliest pioneers of what became known as 'rough stuff' hailed from the North. A. W. Rumsey of Keswick and Albert Winstanley of Bolton are just two whose articles, books and photographs captured the pleasures of the path less pedalled. In the 1950s a group of like-minded cyclists founded the Rough-Stuff Fellowship as the world's first off-road cycling club. This was decades before the plaid-shirted hippies in California rode their clunkers down the hills of Marin County. The club has always had a strong presence in the North and anyone with an interest in this area of cycling history should look up RSF Archive's feed on Instagram. The lesson of the RSF for cyclists of today is you don't have to be a daredevil mountain biker or own a big-tyred bike with full suspension to enjoy heading off-road. All that's needed is a sense of adventure and not to be

in too much of a hurry. As Bob Harrison, an RSF founder member who took brilliant photographs of his rough stuff exploits, liked to say, "I never go for a walk without my bike".

These routes all take in sections of rough stuff, some longer than others, though there is almost always an alternative for those who prefer tarmac.

No. 4 LIQUID LANDSCAPE

Even the smallest roads in the Lake District can get busy, especially during the summer. This route takes in a couple of excellent introductory sections of rough stuff that get you away from the cars, and give a new perspective on the landscape. The first are a couple of byways that skirt the edges of Mosser Fell and Whin Fell and the other is a short downhill section through Wythop Woods.

No. 11 INTO THE WILD

Northumberland's vast expanses of forestry plantations have the biggest network of American-style gravel tracks in the North, right the way across the Kielder, Wark and Redesdale forests. This ride takes in the well-groomed and family-friendly Lakeside Way, as well as the lonely miles of the Forest Drive and Pennine Way.

No. 13 PURPLE HAZE

Most of this route is on good, unsurfaced tracks, linked by quiet lanes. The first section across Fylingdales Moor, within sight of the top-secret military radar station, is good gravel double track along some ancient medieval routes through forests and heather-clad moors. The second section is the Cinder Track, an old railway path that is overdue a surface upgrade but is quite rideable on a touring bike.

Kielder Forest

Mastiles Lane

Mosser Fell

No. 20 UP HILL DOWN DALE

Mastiles Lane is a rough stuff classic. It's a green lane that runs from Malham Tarn to Kilnsey in the Yorkshire Dales. This route takes in a short section, just enough to give a taste, though you could incorporate almost the entire length of it by tweaking the route a little.

No. 22 SECRETS OF SWALEDALE

This route includes an option for a short but utterly bewitching rough stuff section in Upper Swaledale. It passes hay meadows, atmospheric ruins, and a river gorge with some big waterfalls.

No. 27 WHERE THERE'S MUCK

Rough stuff is that much more satisfying when it is on the doorstep of a big city. There are some excellent rough stuff interludes on this route around the attractive rural backwaters and post-industrial edgelands between Sheffield, Rotherham and Barnsley.

No. 29 TAKE THE HIGH ROAD

The outbound half of this ride includes the long and winding Hornby Road, quite possibly the best moorland track in the North and one of the best-kept cycling secrets of the Forest of Bowland.

Hornby Road

CUMBRIA &
THE LAKES

POETRY IN MOTION

An intimate journey into the heart of Lakeland taking
in some of its best-loved lakes and tarns

———

For the steady stream of Romantic poets and their admirers who made the journey to Dove Cottage, the damp, cramped home where William Wordsworth and his sister Dorothy spent eight years of "plain living, but high thinking", the road from Ambleside was the finishing straight of a journey that might have taken several days or more. The likes of Samuel Taylor Coleridge and Thomas De Quincey would have walked along the road, but today's A591 is so busy with motor traffic that it's fit for neither walking nor cycling. The car is a modern development that would have shocked, and likely horrified, the sensitive, poetic souls who came to the Lakes as an escape from the noise and the stink of city life at the start of the Industrial Revolution.

There is a good alternative route in the form of a quiet lane and an off-road track on the far side of Rydal Water and Grasmere, from where there are sublime views across to Nab Scar and Heron Pike. Grasmere heaves with tourists but it is a short detour off the route if you want to make the pilgrimage to Dove Cottage (an essential port of call for any Wordsworth fan Ⓐ). After this gentle lakeside warm-up, the hard riding begins with a lung-busting climb up Red Bank and over to Great Langdale. This is one of the Lake District's great mountain crucibles, with the jagged line of the Langdale Pikes dominat-

ing the skyline. There's plenty of time to savour the view on the stiff climb out of the valley. At the top, in a hanging valley between Great and Little Langdale, is Blea Tarn Ⓑ. Wordsworth described it in *The Excursion*, "A quiet treeless nook, with two green fields, a liquid pool that glittered in the sun, and one bare dwelling; one abode, no more!" This was the dwelling place of Wordsworth's The Solitary, a man so plagued by loss and tragedy that he chose to live apart from society. The house is still there and the tarn is swimmable on a fine day.

Little Langdale sits at the foot of Wrynose Pass, a connecting route to Ride No. 2 and the Western Lakes. A good bridleway leads through the woods towards Coniston. Along the way are remnants of old mines and slate quarries and it's well worth turning right just after the ford to take a look at Cathedral Cave Ⓒ, a spectacular chamber in an old slate quarry. Leave your bikes at the bottom of the path but take a bike light with you in case you want to venture deeper.

After rejoining the road in High Tilberthwaite, look out for Touchstone Fold Ⓓ, a slate sheepfold made by the artist Andy Goldsworthy. He is best known for his installations out of rocks, ice, leaves or branches, which he photographs as they change with the passage of time and the force of

---

START & FINISH: Ambleside • DISTANCE: 33 miles / 54km • TOTAL ASCENT: 890m
TERRAIN: Mostly lanes, a few sections of good gravel track. Moderate.

the elements. "It's not about art," he has explained. "It's just about life and the need to understand that a lot of things in life do not last." This is one of 46 sheepfold installations that Goldsworthy and his helpers have built in Cumbria.

Coniston sits at the head of Coniston Water; with the sun in the south it is a five-mile-long sheet of shimmering silver. Two names rise above all others in the history of Coniston: John Ruskin and Donald Campbell.

Ruskin, a leading art critic and public intellectual of Victorian Britain, once said that "nature is painting for us, day after day, pictures of infinite beauty if only we have the eyes to see them". Ruskin loved the Lakes and spent the last three decades of his life at Brantwood, a house two miles south of the village, with infinitely beautiful views across the lake to Coniston Old Man.

Donald Campbell was more into speed than scenery. He set world water speed records here but died in a crash while attempting to top 300 mph in 1967. His body and his jet-powered motorboat Bluebird K7 lay on the lake bed for years until divers recovered them in 2001. Both Ruskin and Campbell are buried in Coniston churchyard. The small museum in the village contains reams of Ruskin ephemera, salvaged pieces of Campbell's Bluebird and evidence that Coniston was the setting and inspiration for Arthur Ransome's *Swallows and Amazons* stories.

There's a good swim spot just beyond the village on a track down to the Coniston Ferry Landing Ⓔ, and another on the roadside by the turning for the Monk Coniston car park Ⓕ.

Next, the route follows the back way to Tarn Hows Ⓖ. It is a wildly popular Lakeland beauty spot.

It looks entirely natural, untouched by human hand, but that's an illusion. It's really a managed landscape, the product of late Victorian imaginations. The trees were planted and the tarn is formed by a downstream dam. It didn't look at all like this in Wordsworth's day. The site is owned by the National Trust thanks largely to Beatrix Potter, who was a staunch early supporter of the Trust. From Knipe Fold there's an option of a short cut back to Ambleside, or else the route heads south via Hawkshead. The village is home to the Beatrix Potter Gallery Ⓗ and, at the far end of Esthwaite Water, Hill Top Ⓘ, the house where she lived (both NT, £). It's a steep hill down to Windermere and the traffic-free lakeshore track, which passes the absurd Gothic Revival castle at Wray Ⓙ (NT, £). For the final miles back to Ambleside there's the welcome option of a traffic-free gravel path beside the B5286 which, like many roads in the Lakes, can be busy with cars and coaches at weekends and in the summer.

PUBS & PIT STOPS

OLD DUNGEON GHYLL HOTEL, Great Langdale LA22 9JY (015394 37272) Historic Lakeland hotel with a famous hikers' bar.

THREE SHIRES INN, Little Langdale LA22 9NZ (015394 37215) Country pub with rooms.

Plenty of choice in Coniston: **THE SUN INN** (LA21 8HQ, 015394 41248), just up the hill, has a south-facing terrace overlooking the lake; **HERDWICKS** (LA21 8DU, 015394 41141) and **THE GREEN HOUSEKEEPER** (LA21 8DU, 015394 41925) serve good-value, freshly cooked lunches, as does the spacious, glass-fronted **BLUEBIRD CAFÉ** (LA21 8AN, 015394 41649) right by the boating centre on the lakeshore.

TOWER BANK ARMS, Near Sawrey LA22 0LF (015394 36334) Comfortable B&B with a good bar.

DRUNKEN DUCK INN, Barngates LA22 0NG (015394 36347) Great foodie pub with stylish rooms, worth a detour.

GANDHI'S CAFÉ, The Slack, Ambleside LA22 9DQ Home-cooked vegetarian and vegan food.

TARN FOOT FARM CAMPSITE, Loughrigg LA22 9HF (015394 32596) Rustic campsite by a swimming lake, no showers.

BIKE SHOP: Ghyllside Cycles, The Slack, Ambleside LA22 9DQ (015394 33592) Bike hire available.

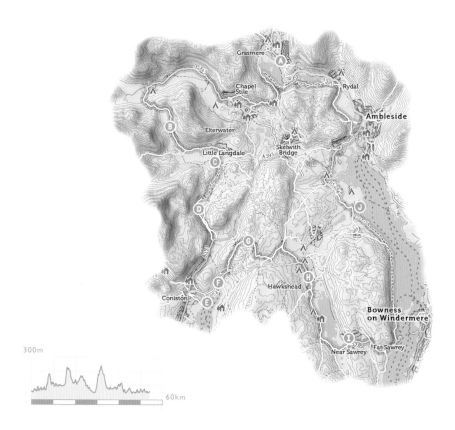

Grasmere

Chapel
Stile

Rydal

Ambleside

Elterwater

Little Langdale

Skelwith
Bridge

Coniston

Hawkshead

Bowness
on Windermere

Near Sawrey   Far Sawrey

300m

60km

Coniston Water

Langdale Pikes

STILL GLIDES THE STREAM

Escape the crowds in Wordsworth's beloved Duddon Valley,
and test your legs on the infamous Hardknott Pass

———

As early as 1793, Wordsworth had informed his readers that, though "very rarely visited", the Duddon Valley contained "some of the most romantic scenery of these mountains". He found the valley so lovely that he wrote a series of 35 sonnets about it, a kind of lyrical guidebook. His friend Coleridge exclaimed in a notebook, "O lovely lovely Vale!" and Turner followed them here and painted the vast and treacherous expanses of sand where the river empties into the Irish Sea. Back then it was a rarely visited part of the lakes. That's still true today, and it's every bit as lovely as Wordsworth described it. The Duddon isn't a long river and while Wordsworth took his readers from source to sea, this ride follows the river upstream before heading over Hardknott Pass into Eskdale and a return over the lonely landscape of Birker Fell.

The nearest train station is at Foxfield, hard by the Duddon Mosses National Nature Reserve, one of England's few remaining peatland habitats, a remnant of the retreating glaciers that carved out the valleys of the Lakes, and home to dozens of rare plant and animal species Ⓐ. Broughton-in-Furness is a tiny market town with a good bakery for stocking up on snacks and picnic supplies; there's not much available on the route until Eskdale.

Much of the valley is covered with long pockets of broadleaf woodland. Beautiful at any time of year, they are at their most spectacular in autumn, with every leaf aflame. In spring many of the woods shimmer with iridescent carpets of bluebells. As well as the patchwork of ancient woodland there are 1930s and 40s conifer plantations that the Forestry Commission is gradually clearing and regenerating with native species.

Though the Duddon Valley has been inhabited all the way back to the Neolithic Age, its inhabitants engaged in industries like slate quarrying, copper mining, iron smelting, peat extraction and cloth manufacturing, there are no settlements of any size beyond the hamlets of Ulpha and Seathwaite. There are good swim spots at Duddon Bridge Ⓑ, from the neatly trimmed grass riverbank by humpbacked Ulpha Bridge Ⓒ, and further up the valley at Birks Bridge Ⓓ. On a fine, sunny day after a picnic and a paddle in the river you may be moved to compose a sonnet.

Most of the place names here are derived from the Old Norse language, and Ulpha is thought to mean 'the hill frequented by wolves'. Two miles further on is Seathwaite, 'clearing of the sedges', a hamlet with a pub dating back to the 17th century. Wordsworth is known to have

---

START & FINISH: Broughton • DISTANCE: 31 miles / 50km • TOTAL ASCENT: 1063m
TERRAIN: Lanes and two short sections of A-road. Challenging.

Ulpha Bridge

Dale Head

stopped at the Newfield Inn for refreshment and a bed for the night. Seathwaite is at the western end of the Walna Scar Road, an unsurfaced byway that's one of the great British rough stuff cycling and mountain biking routes. It climbs the southern spurs of the Coniston Old Man before descending to Coniston. Our route, however, keeps to the surfaced road and follows on up the valley, passing the aptly named Froth Pot waterfalls before passing through ridiculously picturesque 17th-century Dale Head Farm before arriving at the hamlet of Cockley Beck and its packhorse bridge Ⓔ.

Wrynose Bottom is a glacial valley straight out of a geography book. It is bookended by two of the great road climbs of the British Isles. Wrynose Pass leads over to Little Langdale (and Ride No.

1), but our route makes a left turn up Hardknott Pass. A 1911 cycling guidebook described the road as "difficult going West, cruel coming East". Since then it's been upgraded with a tarmac surface which, at 1-in-3 sections, appears to be gently sliding down the hillside. In the 13th century the pass was known as Wainscarth, or 'cart gap', which shows it was used by vehicles back then. As you're battling your way up, remember that this is actually the easier of the two sides. Once you're at the top, resist the temptation to fly straight down the other side; stop to walk up to the Hardknott Roman fort which is about halfway down, on the right-hand side Ⓕ. To my mind this is the most impressive Roman relic in Britain, better even than Hadrian's Wall. It was built around 130AD to guard the route from the harbour at Ravenglass to forts at Ambleside and Penrith. When a bleak wind is roaring up the valley, and the rain is hammering down in sheets it's hard not to feel for the poor legionnaires stationed here for years on end. Then again, archaeologists have discovered the remains of a bathhouse, so it seems they had the basic comforts covered.

The run along Eskdale comes as a relief after the big climb and there is a good run of pubs and cafés here as well as an excellent watermill at Boot Ⓖ. Comprising a collection of ramshackle stone buildings across a packhorse bridge, it's the last remaining working water-powered corn mill in the Lake District. Tours are available, though check in advance for opening times (£). Just past

Boot, Dalegarth is the terminus of the Ravenglass and Eskdale heritage steam railway. Getting back to the Duddon Valley means another climb, this time by the ancient way over Birker Fell, one of the most isolated parts of the Lakes. It's known to be ancient because there are remains of a Bronze Age settlement and field system at Devoke Water Ⓗ. Just above the lake, the farmstead at Woodend is thought to be a very early Quaker settlement.

Back in the Duddon Valley the route then takes an alternative way back from Ulpha to Broughton, past the old quarries below Stickle Pike and down into the Lickle Valley via the remarkable and utterly unspoilt Blacksmiths Arms pub in Broughton Mills.

PUBS & PIT STOPS

BROUGHTON VILLAGE BAKERY, LA20 6HQ (01229 716284) Bread, pies, cakes and a small café.

NEWFIELD INN, Seathwaite LA20 6ED (01229 716208) Cosy whitewashed inn, food served all day.

THE WOOLPACK INN, Eskdale CA19 1TH (019467 23230) Pub, café and B&B. Good food.

BROOK HOUSE INN, Boot, Eskdale CA19 1TG (019467 23288) Pub with rooms.

THE BOOT INN, Boot, Eskdale CA19 1TG (019467 23711) Pub with rooms.

YHA ESKDALE, CA19 1TH (0345 371 9317) Small, stone-built hostel with small campsite.

BOWER HOUSE INN, Eskdale CA19 1TD (019467 23244) Just off-route, cheery inn with rooms.

KING GEORGE IV INN, Eskdale CA19 1TS (019467 23470) Nice locals' pub with B&B and a self-catering flat. Food served all day.

WOODEND, Birker Fell LA20 6DY (019467 23277) Lovely B&B and cottages up high on the wild fells.

BLACKSMITHS ARMS, Broughton Mills LA20 6AX (01229 716824) Wonderful rural pub. Local ales and good food.

BIKE SHOP: West Lakes Adventure, Boot CA19 1TH (019467 23753) Mountain bike hire.

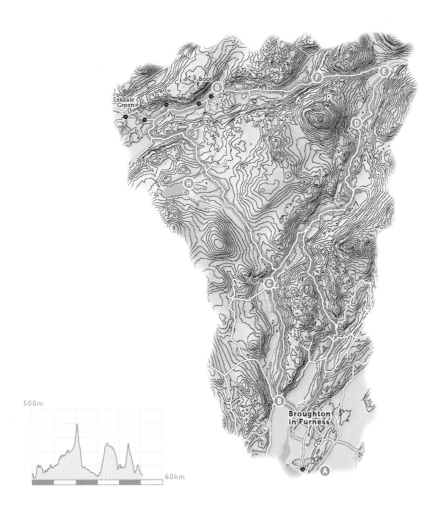

500m

60km

Hardknott Pass

Roman Fort, Hardknott

Birker Fell

Hardknott Pass

Duddon Valley

MOUNTAIN HIGH

From the Irish Sea coast to the shore of England's deepest lake
and the foot of England's highest peak

————

The peaks of the Lake District seem much higher than they really are. Partly it's their craggy and vertiginous forms, partly it's because of the way they rise dramatically from the sea. Scafell Pike is England's highest peak but is just ten miles as the crow flies from the coast.

This ride begins in Ravenglass, a small, sleepy hamlet on a large natural harbour at the confluence of the rivers Esk, Irt and Mite. When the Romans were here it was a much busier place with shipyards and a port servicing the interior via the fort at Hardknott and onwards to the Pennines. Almost nothing remains other than a tumbledown bathhouse Ⓐ, which isn't a patch on the magnificent ruins at Hardknott (see Ride No. 2).

The ride is pancake-flat across the flood plain as the forbidding forms of the western fells come into view on the horizon. Up a dead end lane and surrounded by nothing but a few farmsteads seems an odd place for a church, but St Paul's, Irton, is worth a stop Ⓑ. The church is Victorian and contains some stained glass designed by Edward Burne-Jones and manufactured by William Morris, but the site is of much greater antiquity. The 3-metre-high stone cross in the churchyard is over a thousand years old. In the 9th century, a time when most buildings and many churches would have been made from timber, a cross made from stone was an expression of prestige and permanence. Another even bigger such cross can be found further on in the ride at Gosforth Ⓔ, dated to a century later. The Irton cross is carved in the Irish Celtic Christian tradition, while the Gosforth cross has strong Scandinavian influences, with an intermingling of Norse mythology. Together they show the power of successive outside influences on the culture of Northern England. If you want to compare them side by side there are replicas of both in the Victoria and Albert Museum in London. Besides the cross, the church at Gosforth contains a pair of hogback tombs, more visual evidence of Viking settlers in Cumbria.

At Santon Bridge the road begins to climb, and the views just get better and better. Emerging from the woods around Wasdale Hall (now a Youth Hostel) you are confronted by the Wasdale Screes Ⓒ – a dark rampart of shattered rock buttresses one-third of a mile high that disgorges an almost vertical boulder field into the water. Wast Water is more Norwegian fjord than English lake. Perhaps it made the Norse settlers feel at home. As well as stone crosses and tombs, they left their mark on the way Cumbrians name the landscape. The word fell (meaning hill) derives from Old Norse. So too do beck (stream), foss (waterfall), gill (ravine), howe (hill), thwaite (clearing) and tarn (small lake) among many others.

START & FINISH: Ravenglass • DISTANCE: 29 miles / 47km • TOTAL ASCENT: 441m
TERRAIN: All lanes. Easy.

Irton cross

Gosforth cross

This is an extreme landscape and is fitting that it should have produced a man universally agreed to be the greatest fell runner of all time. Joss Naylor was born at Wasdale Head in 1936 and left school at 15 to work on the family farm. Chronic back injuries meant he was deemed unfit for National Service, but sheep farming in Lakeland breeds a special kind of toughness as well as an affinity with the fells. Naylor entered his first fell race at the age of 24 and went on to win races and set records throughout the 1970s and 80s. His 24-hour Lakeland record run saw him bag 72 peaks, covering over a hundred miles and an Everest-and-a-half of vertical ascent. Aged 50, he ran the Wainwrights (the 214 peaks of the Lake District) in seven days – a record that stood for 28 years. His fastest time up and down Scafell Pike is 47 minutes, and he doubts it will ever be beaten. Most walkers take about four hours so it's quite doable in midsummer if you leave your bike at the bottom. A living legend of the Lake District, 'Iron Joss' is now in his eighties and still keeps sheep in Wasdale.

From Wasdale Head Ⓓ the only onward routes are the extreme rough routes of Black Sail and Sty Head passes, so the ride retraces the route back along Wast Water. Reaching depths of 80m (15m below sea level), its icy waters have held dark secrets. In 1984 divers discovered the body of a woman murdered eight years previously, her skin preserved like wax due to the lack of oxygen. Less macabre are the gnome gardens built by recreational divers. Police removed them after a spate of deaths among divers trying to find them. Rumour has it that they've been reinstated deeper than the 50m that police are permitted to dive.

The lake is also the main source of water for the nearby Sellafield nuclear complex. A reliable supply of water for cooling the reactors was a big part of the reason why Europe's largest nuclear facility was established here in the late-1940s. Initially built to make plutonium for the atom bomb, the site is now the place where hazardous nuclear waste material from around Europe comes to be processed and stored. It's a long game – plutonium remains hazardous for 100,000 years, and plans for 'permanent' deep storage in caverns beneath the Lake District National Park have stoked renewed controversy.

Sellafield currently employs around 10,000 people and most locals think the benefit of these jobs outweighs the small but measurable increased incidence of cancer in the population. It could have been very much worse. In 1957 a reactor caught fire and a Chernobyl-style meltdown was narrowly averted. It would have made the West Cumbria and the Lake District uninhabitable for thousands of years.

From Gosforth there's a good cycle path beside the B5344 to Seascale, from where coastal cycle path NCR 72 gives the option of a closer look at Sellafield (Ⓕ a detour of two miles north) before returning to Ravenglass.

PUBS & PIT STOPS

BRIDGE INN, Santon Bridge CA19 1UX (019467 26221) Large pub with rooms, food served all day.

THE STRANDS INN, Nether Wasdale CA20 1ET (019467 26237) Friendly village pub and microbrewery. Rooms.

CHURCH STILE FARM, Nether Wasdale CA20 1ET (019467 26252) Farm shop selling local produce on a large and well-equipped campsite with glamping options.

YHA WASDALE HALL, CA20 1ET (019467 26222) Hostel in a rather grand lakeside manor house.

WASDALE HEAD INN, Wasdale Head CA20 1EX (019467 26229) Large walkers' inn with neighbouring farm B&B.

NATIONAL TRUST CAMPSITE, Wasdale Head CA20 1EX (015394 32733) Campsite beside Wast Water.

BURNTHWAITE FARM, Wasdale Head CA20 1EX (019467 26242) Remote farmhouse B&B right below Great Gable.

LION AND LAMB, Gosforth CA20 1AL (019467 58422) Village pub with rooms serving good, reasonably priced food.

WILD OLIVE, Gosforth CA20 1AH (019467 25999) Italian café serving wood-fired pizzas.

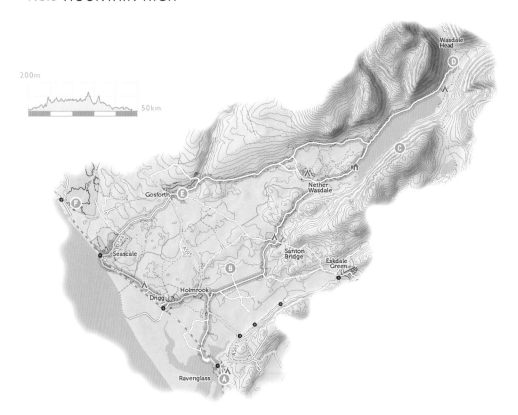

Hogback tombstones, Gosforth

Wast Water

LIQUID LANDSCAPE

Rivers, lakes and waterfalls, two great Lakeland pubs and bit of rough stuff

———

Rough stuff cycling is part of the fabric of Lakeland and hardy, adventurous cyclists have been carrying on where the good road ends since the 1890s. It was especially in vogue in the 1930s and 1940s. The Rough-Stuff Fellowship was founded in the 1950s as the first cycling club devoted to off-road riding. The splendour of the scenery, the wealth of off-road tracks, the generous provision of youth hostel accommodation and the traditional tolerance for low-key wild camping made the Lakes a perfect destination for rough stuff cycling, and none of that has changed. Heading off-road opens up new possibilities for wayfaring in the wildest, most mountainous parts of Lakeland. Classic pass-storming routes like Black Sail, Styhead, Gatescarth, High Street, Esk Hause and Rossett Gill are proper challenges and beyond the scope of this book, as they include long sections of pushing and even carrying your bike (but don't let that put you off, if you're feeling adventurous). This ride gives a taste of the pleasures of rough stuff cycling in the Lakes with three short off-road sections. If you prefer to stick to the tarmac throughout, that's fine as there are ways to avoid the rough stuff entirely.

Starting at Keswick, the route heads west around the head of Derwent Water into the Newlands Valley. It follows the Newlands Beck all the way to the pass at Newlands Hause (*hause* is a regional dialect word for pass or ridge) Ⓐ. It's a beautiful climb, with views up to Moss Force (*force* means waterfall). Samuel Taylor Coleridge came here in the summer of 1802 and his description fills two pages of his notebook and, as one of the truly great pieces of outdoor writing, it is worth quoting at length: "Great masses of water, one after the other, that in twilight one might have feelingly compared them to a vast crowd of huge white bears, rushing one over the other against the wind – their long white hair shattering abroad in the wind… What a sight it is to look down on such a cataract! – the wheels, that circumvolve in it – the leaping up and plunging forward of that infinity of pearls and glass bulbs – the continual change of the Matter, the perpetual sameness of the Form..." Much depends on whether the beck is in spate or not. After heavy rain it's every bit as Coleridge described.

When he came this way, Coleridge noted the contrast between the "exceeding greenness & pastoral beauty" of the Newlands Valley with "savage wildness of the mountains". As you crest the pass you can immediately grasp what he was getting at. The monstrous ridge of Crag Hill is dark, desolate and treeless, so thoroughly terrifying that it's a relief to get down among the

---

START & FINISH: Keswick • DISTANCE: 34 miles / 55km • TOTAL ASCENT: 972m
TERRAIN: Mostly lanes, optional sections of green lane and forest track. Moderate/Challenging.

Moss Force

Buttermere

dinky stone houses of Buttermere. Here in 1802, the same year that Coleridge was striding around the fells and marvelling at Moss Force, a romantic scandal played out that gripped the nation. Mary Robinson, a beautiful young shepherdess and daughter of the innkeeper of the Fish Inn, met and married a man presenting himself as The Hon. Colonel Alexander Augustus Hope, a Scottish MP and brother of an earl. Colonel Hope was soon revealed to be an imposter and a bigamist who had left a trail of broken hearts, abandoned wives and fatherless children all across England. He was tried for forgery and hanged the following year. The plight of Mary, the Maid of Buttermere, made national news – a melodrama of innocence and scandal, tainted love, rank deception and class transgression touched all the big taboos of the time. The story was retold in a novel by Cumbrian author and broadcaster Melvyn Bragg.

Buttermere, Crummock Water and Loweswater were once one large lake all carved by the same glacier, but now each has its own character. The road along the lakeside is as joyous a ride as any I know. Buttermere is the perfect swimmer's lake, with an excellent path around its entire perimeter and no motorised craft allowed. At the corner nearest the village is a small shingle beach Ⓑ with views across to Fleetwith Pike and Haystacks. Crummock Water is bigger and feels wilder. Wood House Beach is a good swim spot, accessible on a footpath to the left of the road immediately as you reach the lake Ⓒ.

On the lowland between Crummock Water and Loweswater is the Kirkstile Inn which has everything you could want from a country pub. From the northern shore of Loweswater the first of the ride's three brief rough stuff interludes climbs the edge of Mosser Fell Ⓓ, followed by a second across Whin Fell Ⓔ. Clearly visible to the north is the Georgian town of Cockermouth where William Wordsworth was born and spent his "sweet childish days". From Low Lorton there are two options for the final leg of the ride back to Keswick. The first is via the Whinlatter Pass Ⓕ, which is shorter but hillier and entirely on road. It passes the popular mountain bike centre in Whinlatter Forest which has more than twenty miles of graded trails from gentle gravel to moderate, challenging and severe. The second is the longer, more scenic and less hilly route via Wythop Mill Ⓖ. Both are good but if time allows I prefer the latter, which includes two miles on rough stuff tracks through the woods and the option of a short detour to the historic bar of the Pheasant Inn on Bassenthwaite Lake. The routes converge at Braithwaite from where NCR 71 leads back to Keswick.

PUBS & PIT STOPS

LITTLETOWN FARM, CA12 5TU (017687 78353) Rustic tearoom and B&B in the Newlands Valley.

THE FISH INN, Buttermere CA13 9XA (017687 70253) Historic Buttermere inn.

YHA BUTTERMERE, CA13 9XA (0345 371 9508) Hostel in a grand Victorian house with glamping and camping.

SYKE FARM TEA ROOM, Buttermere CA13 9XA (017687 70277) Airy café in an old tractor shed, basic campsite.

KIRKSTILE INN, Loweswater CA13 0RU (01900 85219) Glorious old inn with roaring fires and hearty food. Rooms.

LORTON VILLAGE SHOP, High Lorton CA13 9UL (01900 85102) Village shop selling picnic provisions from local suppliers.

WHEATSHEAF INN, Low Lorton CA13 9UW (01900 85199) Pub with rooms and campsite.

PHEASANT INN, Bassenthwaite Lake CA13 9YE (017687 76234) Two miles off-route, a rambling old coaching inn with a terrific bar.

BIKE SHOP: Keswick Bikes, 133 Main Street, Keswick CA12 5NJ (017687 75202) Bike hire available.

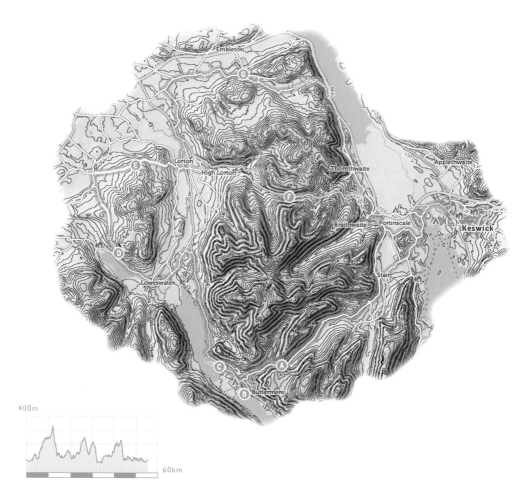

Kirkstile Inn

Mosser Fell

Darling Fell

Newlands Valley

Crummock Water

BACK O' SKIDDA

A circuit of the Skiddaw massif from bustling Keswick
to the solitude of the Caldbeck Fells

———

Keswick is the biggest town in the northern Lake District and Skiddaw is Keswick's mountain. It's the third-highest mountain in England but a purposeful walker can be up and back from the town centre in three hours. These days Keswick is best known as a centre for outdoor pursuits but it was once world-renowned for the manufacture of pencils, thanks to the discovery in 1565 of a uniquely large deposit of solid graphite a few miles away in the Borrowdale Fells. At first the sticks of graphite were wrapped in sheepskin, until someone had the bright idea of encasing them in wood, and the pencil was born. For centuries it was a cottage industry of independent craftsmen until a factory was opened in 1832. The Derwent Pencil Museum Ⓐ tells the full story and its displays include the world's largest pencil which weighs in at nearly half a tonne.

Skiddaw, a dark, unruly heap of a mountain, is difficult to make out from the valley floor but, together with its neighbour Blencathra to the east and the Caldbeck Fells to the north, it comprises a single block of mountain country through which no paved road passes. This ride is a circuit of Skiddaw, but it is possible to ride into the heart of the massif – Back o' Skidda – where there's a remote, off-grid hostel and campsite where you can stay overnight. More on that later.

The route out of Keswick follows the Sustrans coast-to-coast cycle route on an old railway line, large sections of which were washed away by floods during Storm Desmond in 2015. The route will be reinstated eventually, but in the meantime there's a diversion uphill via the stone circle at Castlerigg Ⓑ which is ample reward for the effort of the climb. The circle consists of around 40 mean-looking, tooth-shaped boulders. At around 5,000 years old, it is among the oldest stone circles in Europe and quite possibly the most sublime in terms of setting: on a large level plateau, it floats over Borrowdale with mighty Blencathra rising above. The cosmic alignment of the stones attests to the astronomical knowledge of the Late Neolithic / Early Bronze Age people who built it. What function it served, what people did here, nobody really knows.

The first village on the circuit is Threlkeld – a Norse name if ever there was one – which is sandwiched between the lower slopes of Blencathra and the River Glenderaterra (both these names are Cumbric in origin – the old and now extinct Celtic language of the North, closely related to Welsh). Threlkeld is an old mining and slate quarrying town, and across the A66 is a volunteer-run museum which offers underground tours into a reconstructed lead and copper mine Ⓒ (£).

START & FINISH: Keswick • DISTANCE: 33 miles / 53km • TOTAL ASCENT: 771m
TERRAIN: Lanes and one short section of railway trail. Easy.

Threlkeld is one of four places on the route from where it's possible to ride into the interior of the Skiddaw massif and stop in at Skiddaw House. This, formerly a gamekeepers' and shepherds' refuge, is now a remote off-grid hostel Ⓓ. To get there, follow the road to the Blencathra Field Centre and keep going. Even though this is the easiest of the ways in, it's rough-going in places so be prepared for some walking as well as riding.

After a short, noisy stretch on a cycle path beside the A66 to Scales, the route continues around the mountain and along some of the quietest lanes in the whole of the Lake District. Cumbria is the birthplace of Quakerism, and Mungrisdale and Mosedale were early outposts. The Friends Meeting House in Mosedale dates from 1702 and is still in use Ⓔ. In July and August it opens up as a coffee shop, selling home-made soups, teas and cakes for a local charity. From Mosedale there's another route to Skiddaw House, on a bridleway following the River Caldew.

Leaving the high country behind for a short while, the route descends to the pretty villages of Hesket Newmarket and Caldbeck and a possible link with Ride No. 7 to Carlisle and the Solway Plain.

The Caldbeck Fells were a centre of mining for centuries and are now a magnet for amateur geologists who hunt for specimens of unusual minerals among the spoil from the old mines. It's then more lakeland lanes around the final corner of the Skiddaw massif and the last and most rideable route to Skiddaw House (the bridleway starts opposite Peter House Farm near Bassenthwaite Ⓕ).

The route passes close to Bassenthwaite Lake but it's worth a small detour for a better view. One stunning spot is the ancient lakeside church of

St Bega, accessible down a well-signposted track on the right ⓖ. Another good viewpoint is courtesy of the Lake District Osprey Project in Dodd Wood, accessible from the Old Sawmill Tearoom on the A591 ⓗ. Ospreys began nesting here in 2001, the first to breed in the Lakes for 150 years. With a five-foot wingspan, the birds are quite something to watch in flight. They are best spotted between April and August. The project has a lower viewpoint near the road, which is also good for spotting red squirrels. You can cycle half a mile up through the forest to the Upper Viewpoint which is where you're more likely to see an osprey. High-powered telescopes and binoculars are provided.

A two-mile section of the A-road is sadly unavoidable and the final run in to Keswick through Applethwaite has good views up to the summit of Skiddaw and down across Derwent Water.

PUBS & PIT STOPS

THRELKELD COFFEE SHOP, Threlkeld CA12 4RX (017687 79501) Community-run café in the village hall.

MILL INN, Mungrisdale CA11 0XR (017687 79632) Brewery-owned pub with rooms. Food served all day.

THE OLD CROWN, Hesket Newmarket CA7 8JG (016974 78288) Community-owned village pub. Pub grub at lunchtimes and evenings.

Plenty of choice in Caldbeck: WATERMILL CAFÉ (CA7 8DR, 016974 78267) and OLD SMITHY TEA ROOM (CA7 8DY, 016974 78378) serve light lunches and cakes; CALDBECK CAMPING (CA7 8DS, 016974 78367) is a small site by the river and the KIRKLAND STORE (CA7 8EA, 016974 78252) sells basic provisions.

SNOOTY FOX, Uldale CA7 1HA (016973 71479) Just off-route, country pub with rooms. Food served all day.

RAVENSTONE MANOR HOTEL, Bassenthwaite CA12 4QG (017687 76240) Comfortable Victorian country house hotel.

SKIDDAW HOUSE, CA12 4QX (07747 174293) Off-grid mountain hostel, booking essential.

FELLPACK, 19 Lake Rd, Keswick CA12 5BS (017687 71177) Hip, outdoorsy café serving good simple food and cocktails.

DOG & GUN, 2 Lake Rd, Keswick CA12 5BT (017687 73463) Cosy, bustling pub with great goulash.

BIKE SHOP: Keswick Bikes, 133 Main Street, Keswick CA12 5NJ (017687 75202) Bike hire available.

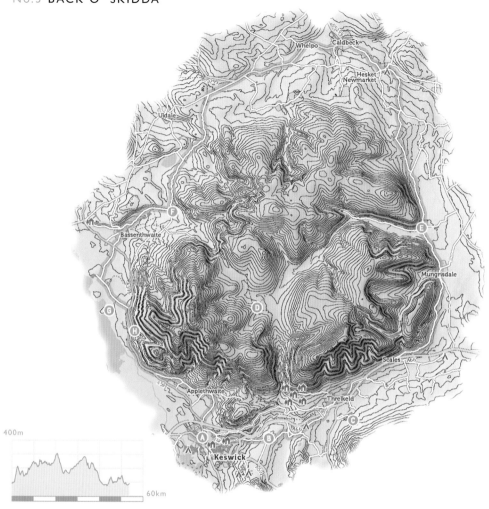

400m

60km

GARDEN OF EDEN

Between the Lakes and the Pennines, an exploration of rolling lands
steeped in history and Britain's highest road climb

———

The River Eden rises in the Yorkshire Dales and enters the sea at the Solway Firth. Its broad valley separates Lakeland from the Pennines and is all good farming land. Appleby is the capital of the old county of Westmorland and makes a good base for exploring a section of the North Pennines that, lacking any roads at all, could claim to be the least-tamed expanse of England. This ride is a freewheeling ramble around the Eden Valley. However, it could take on an altogether more fearsome character if you decide to accept the challenge of the completely optional climb up Great Dun Fell.

The route begins heading west into the north-western extension of the Yorkshire Dales National Park, though this is still very much Cumbria. Like many villages on this ride, Maulds Meaburn is arranged along the road with a stream, a green and common grazing land in the middle. The road climbs steadily from Crosby Ravensworth to cross the A6 on the way to the village of Shap, a key staging point for cyclists riding from Land's End to John o' Groats, as it's just past the highest point in the whole ride. A mile past Shap (and a little off-route) are the ruins of Shap Abbey Ⓐ. In the hills behind Shap Abbey is Sleddale Hall, the farmhouse used in the film *Withnail and I* as Uncle Monty's rural

hideaway Crow Crag. Several scenes from cult classics were filmed in the area.

The route follows the River Lowther all the way to Penrith. Lowther is also the name of a family and you'll find it all around the county, along with Lonsdale, the aristocratic title bestowed on the family. As Cumbria's biggest landowner, the Lowthers owned farms, mines, vast tracts of moorland and slave plantations in the Caribbean. The route passes through Askham, a Lowther estate village, and into the grounds of Lowther Castle Ⓑ. Built in the early 19th century on the site of the older family seat, it had 365 rooms, one for each day of the year. This is where Hugh Lowther, the fifth Earl of Lonsdale, led a lifestyle of ostentatious pleasure on an extreme scale. He loved the colour yellow and maintained a fleet of yellow-painted cars, yellow-liveried servants and musicians, a pack of yellow dogs and a hothouse full of yellow gardenias. He was the founding president of the AA, Automobile Association, which adopted his yellow livery. His extravagance came at a cost: when the Yellow Earl died in 1944 the estate's finances were wrecked and the contents of the castle were sold off in the biggest country house sale of the 20th century.

On inheriting the estate in 1953 James Lowther, the seventh Earl, wanted nothing to do

---

START & FINISH: Appleby • DISTANCE: 58 miles / 93km • TOTAL ASCENT: 1491m
TERRAIN: Lanes, one short section of A-road. Moderate/Challenging.

Shap Abbey

with a place he felt "exemplified gross imperial decadence during a period of abject poverty". As he set about restoring the estate to viability the roofless shell of the castle was used to house livestock. In the early 2000s, a grant-funded restoration project saw the remains of the castle opened to the public as a visitor attraction and it has gone from strength to strength with 130 acres of grounds and gardens and a huge wooden play castle. Walking paths and cycle trails extend for miles into the surrounding countryside. The new generation of Lowthers who run the estate are a more down-to-earth bunch with wholesome passions like fell running and bee-keeping.

From the front of the castle the route follows the old carriage drive through riverside woodland down to Penrith and a sequence of more historic ruins. Brougham Hall has an imposing early Norman gatehouse and a Tudor-era hall Ⓒ. It was largely rebuilt in the 1800s and is being restored once again by local volunteers. There's a café and craft workshops inside. Just across the A6 and off the route are a pair of Neolithic henge monuments – King Arthur's Round Table Ⓓ and Mayburgh Henge Ⓔ. Both are free to enter, and Mayburgh Henge is the larger of the two. They are odd places to stand in, the way they look, and so old. Being such huge structures, they must have been significant for the unknowable people who built them. The enigma of their purpose only adds to the sense of strangeness. The feeling I get here is a bit like vertigo.

Finally, the remains of Brocavum Roman fort and Brougham Castle Ⓕ. Built by the Normans in the 1200s as part of a line of defence against Scottish raiders and cattle rustlers, the castle suffered periods of neglect and reconstruction through the medieval era, eventually falling into permanent decay in the 1700s, just in time to become a picturesque ruin beloved by the Romantics. Wordsworth wrote about exploring it with his sister Dorothy; Turner painted it lit by golden sunbeams after a rainstorm.

From the outskirts of Penrith, the route strikes towards the dark ridge of the Pennines, crossing the River Eden and passing the splendid working watermill at Little Salkeld ⓖ. The short tour led by the miller is highly recommended. The time for a big decision comes just before the village of Knock. Here is the turn for the dead end road that winds its way to the top of Great Dun Fell ⓗ. The climb earns a score of 11 out of 10 from Simon Warren, author of the 100 Climbs guidebooks. On Strava the record time to the top is 23 minutes, but most will take a full hour to get up and back. The giant golf ball at the top is an air traffic control station. The view is as big as you'd expect at 848m above sea level and it's almost always windy. The Helm Wind, the fierce north-easterly which blows here, is the only named wind in the British Isles. The last miles pass through Dufton, one last lovely Cumbrian village, and then back to Appleby.

PUBS & PIT STOPS

Plenty of choice in Appleby: **THE HUB CAFÉ** (CA16 6QR, 017683 51640) serves good, vegetarian-friendly fayre; the **APPLEBY BAKERY** (CA12 5JD, 017687 72257) for picnic materials.

THE BUTCHERS ARMS, Crosby Ravensworth CA10 3JP (01931 715500) Community-owned pub dating back to 1773. Good food.

SHAP CHIPPY, Shap CA10 3JS (01931 716060) Top-notch fish and chips, indoor seating, open lunchtimes and early evening.

CROWN AND MITRE, Bampton Grange CA10 2QR (01931 713225) Country pub with rooms.

KITCHEN GARDEN CAFÉ, Askham Hall CA10 2PF (01931 712350) Sourdough pizza from wood-fired oven, light lunches with fresh, local ingredients.

THE QUEEN'S HEAD, Askham CA10 2PF (01931 712225) Stylish village pub serving outstanding local food.

THE WATERMILL TEAROOM, Little Salkeld CA10 1NN (01768 881523) Organic and vegetarian light lunches and cakes in a ramshackle working mill.

THE STAG INN, Dufton CA16 6DB (017683 51608) Oak-beamed village pub with rooms, superior pub grub.

YHA Dufton CA16 6DB (0345 371 9734) Small, friendly youth hostel.

NEW INN, Brampton CA16 6JS (017683 98991) Rustic, flagstoned free house, weekend carvery.

BIKE SHOPS: HelmWind Cycles, Appleby CA16 6HX (017683 61979); Arragons Cycle Centre, Penrith CA11 7LU (01768 890344) Bike hire available.

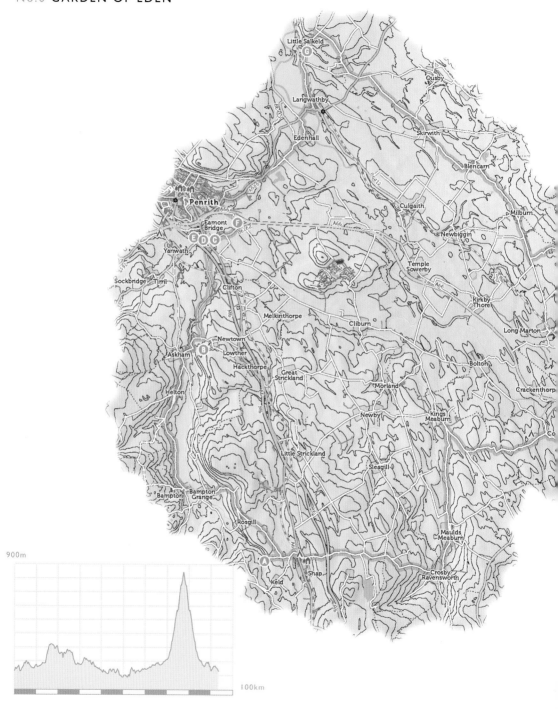

Little Salkeld watermill

Lowther Castle

BORDER RAID

From the border city of Carlisle to the edge of Lakeland and back
via the marshes and mudflats of the Solway Firth

———

The border between England and Scotland, from just north of Carlisle to just north of Berwick, possibly the oldest national land border in the world, though its origins go back to pre-Roman times, was formally agreed in 1237. The people who lived on the border endured centuries of conflict and violence. This was not just between the opposing kingdoms but among lawless clans known as reivers, who conducted violent raids stealing livestock, property and even people, mostly in areas within a day's horse-ride of the border. When the Acts of Union incorporated Scotland and England into the United Kingdom in 1707, Carlisle's character changed from garrison town to industrial city. Textile mills, engineering, railways and food manufacturers all came here. Ginger nuts, bourbons and custard creams are still made here in the McVitie's factory. The city's long story is well told in the excellent Tullie House Museum in the city's Georgian district, right opposite the Norman castle.

Leaving Carlisle's cobbled old quarter, the ride begins gently on the Caldew Cycleway, following the river upstream past old textile mills. Still in operation since 1835, Stead McAlpin of Cummersdale has been printing high-end textiles and has a small factory shop on-site Ⓐ. The cycleway ends at Dalston, another mill town and home to a

Nestlé UK factory which produces nearly a billion sachets of coffee and hot chocolate a year.

Beyond Dalston the route continues to loosely follow the River Caldew into hillier country. By the villages of Hesket Newmarket and Caldbeck, the landscape has changed from flat Solway Plain to the northern fringe of Lakeland. Here the route connects with Ride No. 5 to Keswick. Caldbeck is lovely and it's worth having a wander around on foot, following the path beside the church and along the river. The village's most famous resident is the mountaineer Chris Bonington, a veteran of dozens of Alpine and Himalayan mountains as well as the first to climb the Old Man of Hoy, a precipitous sea stack in the Orkneys that he went up again to mark his 80th birthday.

The climb out of Caldbeck is steep but the higher you go the better the view back across the valley to Caldbeck Fells. Hard to believe but this was once a mining mecca. Geologists have discovered specimens of 160 types of mineral in the hills and it was said that the rich deposits of copper and lead meant Caldbeck Fells was "worth all England else".

At the top of the hill is the Caldbeck TV and radio mast, at 337 metres the third-highest structure in the UK. The road along Faulds Brow is a cracker and it gets better with a six-mile

START & FINISH: Carlisle • DISTANCE: 55 miles / 88km • TOTAL ASCENT: 660m
TERRAIN: All lanes and tarmac cycleway. Moderate.

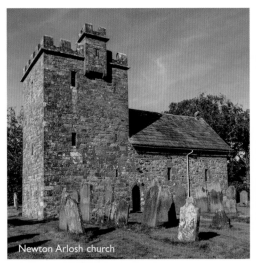

Newton Arlosh church

descent back to near sea level at Wigton, the tough working town and the capital of the Solway Plain. The writer and broadcaster Melvyn Bragg grew up here, living with his family above the Black a Moor Hotel where his father was landlord. On the way out of town just before the railway bridge, look out for the five-storey sandstone windmill that, without its sails, looks like a giant's salt cellar Ⓑ.

After crossing the A596 by the railway steps it's easy riding on quiet lanes through the dairying lands of the Solway Plain, especially if the prevailing south-westerly is blowing. Away to the north, across the marshes and tidal mudflats is a forest of transmitter masts Ⓓ. They broadcast orders to submarines as well as the British national time service which is set by a trio of atomic clocks based at the site.

The remainder of the route follows the Solway coast along the course of Hadrian's Wall. There's almost nothing left to see of the wall itself here, as the masonry has since been reused in more recent buildings, including a number of little

churches that are well worth a visit. The churches at Newton Arlosh Ⓒ and Burgh by Sands Ⓕ are fortified, a common feature in the borders. When under attack by border reivers, people would crowd into the church tower for safety. In one dramatic episode, raiders stole the two bells from the church at Bowness-on-Solway Ⓔ. The raiders, from Annan, were chased across the Solway and threw the bells overboard to hasten their escape. In a reprisal raid local people stole two replacements from Scottish churches across the water. It's a traditional local custom for every new vicar of Annan to ask for their return. Out on the marshes to the north of Burgh by Sands is the place where Edward I, who led brutal military campaigns against the Scottish and Welsh, died of dysentery during a campaign against Robert the Bruce. A memorial marks the spot Ⓖ.

A few miles south of Burgh by Sands, at the disused airfield at Great Orton, another memorial marks a much more recent event that's still raw in local memories. Cumbria was hit hard by the foot-and-mouth epidemic of 2001 and nearly half a million animals – mostly sheep – were brought to the airfield for slaughter and buried in 26 giant trenches. Most of the animals were disease-free but were slaughtered to create a firebreak around infected farms. The site is now a nature reserve but seepage from the decomposing carcasses will have to be monitored for decades Ⓗ.

Just off-route, the small and simple church at Beaumont is built over the site of a Roman turret on the wall Ⓘ. The last part of the ride into Carlisle passes the red-brick colossus of Shaddon Mill Ⓙ. In its day this was the biggest cotton mill in England. It's since been converted into flats but the huge chimney remains a local landmark. Another quirk in Carlisle's history is the nationalisation of its breweries and pubs from 1916 to 1973. The government wanted to control the sale of alcohol to the large number of people working in the city's armaments factories, to reduce drunkenness and potentially disastrous accidents at work. The government commissioned architect Harry Redfern to design thirteen 'New Model Inns' for Carlisle in his distinctive Arts and Crafts style. The Cumberland Inn is the nearest for a post-ride pint.

PUBS & PIT STOPS

HAWKSDALE LODGE, Dalston CA5 7BX (07810 641892) Elegant country house B&B.

WOODSIDE WELCOME CYCLE CAFÉ, Hawksdale near Dalston CA5 7BX (01228 710764) Homespun café serving freshly baked breads, scones and local produce. Weekends only.

THE OLD CROWN, Hesket Newmarket CA7 8JG (016974 78288) Community-owned village pub. Pub grub at lunchtimes and evenings.

Plenty of choice in Caldbeck: **WATERMILL CAFÉ** (016974 78267) and **OLD SMITHY TEA ROOM** (016974 78378) serve light lunches and cakes; **CALDBECK CAMPING** (016974 78367) is a small site by the river and the **KIRKLAND STORES** (016974 78252) sell basic provisions.

BRYCE'S CHIPPY, Wigton CA7 9NJ (016973 44187) Chippy open from 4pm.

JOINERS ARMS, Newton Arlosh CA7 5ET (016973 52669) Unfussy village pub, food served.

PEAR TREE TEA ROOM, Bowness-on-Solway CA7 5AF (07917 131740) Small tea room serving cakes and sandwiches.

HUNTER CAFÉ, Bowness-on-Solway CA7 5AF Tiny café with outdoor seating.

WALLSEND GUEST HOUSE, Bowness-on-Solway CA7 5AF (016973 51055) B&B, tea room and campsite with glamping pods.

Plenty of choice in Carlisle: the **MARKET HALL** (CA3 8QX) for picnic provisions; for after-ride drinks try the **CUMBERLAND INN** (CA1 1QS, 01228 536900), a Harry Redfern designed new model inn, the hip, Bowie-themed **THIN WHITE DUKE** (CA3 8LG, 01228 402334) or the **HOWARD ARMS** (CA3 8ED, 01228 532926) with its spectacular glazed tiles.

BIKE SHOP: Scotby Cycles, Carlisle CA2 5TL (01228 546931); Border City Cycle Hire, Carlisle CA2 5LX (01228 808253) Cycle hire right by the castle.

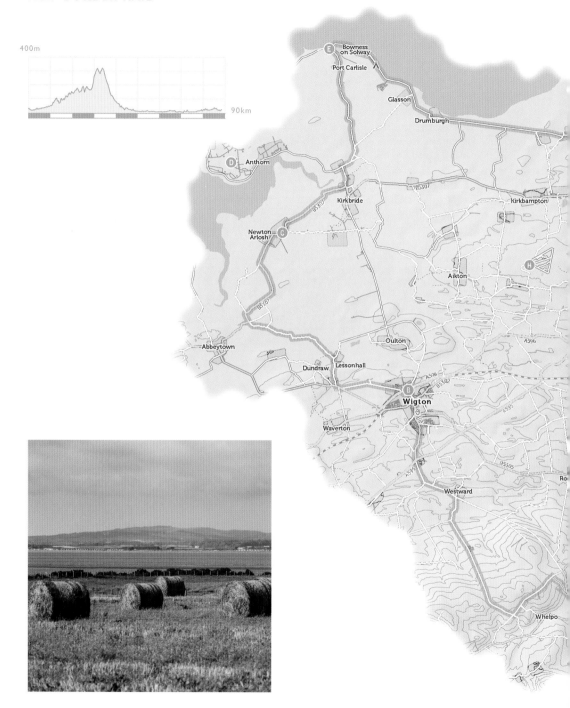

400m

90km

Bowness on Solway

Port Carlisle

Glasson

Drumburgh

Anthorn

Kirkbride

Kirkbampton

B5307

Newton Arlosh

Aikton

Abbeytown

Oulton

A596

Dundraw

Lessonhall

Wigton

A596

B5302

Waverton

B5305

A595

Ro

Westward

A595

Whelpo

THE NORTH EAST

ROOF OF ENGLAND

A big day out in the wind-blown heights of the North Pennines
taking in drovers' roads, waterfalls and old lead mines

———

What the North Pennines lack in photogenic mountain peaks they make up for in high mountain roads. The ridge between the valleys of Weardale and Teesdale boasts the highest road pass in England (Harthope Moss at 627m) and there is an even higher surfaced byway over Coldberry End (674m). This ride takes in their slightly lower neighbour, the Great Southern Drove Road, as well as Yad Moss, Dowgang Hush and Black Hill. All four are 600m above sea level, give or take.

The ride begins in Stanhope which is (just about) accessible by train on the heritage steam line from Bishop Auckland. There are three trains a day most weekends and a few weekdays during the summer. Cycles are welcome on board.

It begins with a gentle warm-up along the valley floor of Weardale before turning left at Westgate onto the Great Southern Drove Road. It's a grand-sounding name for what is today a single-track tarmac lane across the moors. Near the top is the Weardale Ski Club Ⓐ. This is no dry ski slope, it's the real thing as the Pennines sees England's most extreme winter weather. A pair of lifts serve a half-dozen runs with plenty of off-piste routes as well. There are up to 45 skiable days in a winter season, and the weather can be wild at any time of year so it's wise to carry an extra layer, a waterproof and a pair of gloves, even in summer.

A good place to warm up after the descent into Teesdale is the excellent visitor centre and café at Bowlees Ⓑ. Behind it is a half-mile-long path through the woods to the waterfalls of Gibson's Cave. On the other side of the road is a shorter footpath to Low Force, another waterfall and a popular river swim spot – though be prepared as the water is freezing Ⓒ. Bigger but a little harder to get to is High Force Ⓓ.

The next few miles is a long but fairly gentle climb up Teesdale. For my money it's the most beautiful valley in the North Pennines. Away to the left is Cronkley Scar, a wall-like rampart of the Whin Sill, a signature rock formation of the far north. It's a hard rock and so resists erosion. When it does crack it forms sheer cliffs. Hadrian's Wall and the castles of the Northumberland coast are built on prominent outcrops of the Whin Sill. In the Teesdale it is accompanied by a white, crystalline marble known as 'sugar limestone' that has made the valley a botanists' delight of Arctic-Alpine plants, including the bright blue spring gentian.

The road up Teesdale is magnificent, in good part thanks to John Loudon McAdam, the Scottish engineer who did more to advance

---

START & FINISH: Stanhope • DISTANCE: 48 miles / 77km • TOTAL ASCENT: 1479m
TERRAIN: All lanes and quiet B-roads. Very challenging.

Weardale

Teesdale

roadbuilding than anyone since the Romans. Before his time, large rocks or cobbles were laid together with their flat sides up to form a level surface. McAdam proved that this was unnecessary and that a road surface made of a foundation layer of much smaller stones with a thin top layer of even finer stones was cheaper and smoother, and lasted longer. It sounds simple but proved revolutionary. Besides providing a better surface, McAdam's road gave easier and steadier gradients with sweeping, open bends. On the way up, look out for a remnant of the old coaching road, quite primitive by comparison Ⓔ.

On the western horizon are the three Pennine peaks that rise above 800m – Cross Fell, Great Dun Fell and Little Dun Fell – the highest points in England outside the Lake District. Beneath them are the sources of the River Tees and the South Tyne. The summit pass of Yad Moss is the boundary between County Durham and Cumbria, and on the way down there's another ski centre. McAdam's road leads all the way to Alston, but our route takes a short cut over Flinty Fell to Nenthead.

One of the first model villages of the industrial age, Nenthead was built by the Quaker-run London Lead Company. Some of the remains of the smelting works are still there and well worth exploring. True to its radical Quaker roots, the village still has a strong counter-cultural streak. In the early 1980s the 'holy city' hosted three free festivals where New Age travellers and music fans partied to the far-out sounds of the Tibetan Ukrainian Mountain Troupe. The Nenthead moon festivals are but a hazy memory for the select few lucky enough to have been there but as a certified 'dark sky reserve', the North Pennines is still a great place to look up at the night sky. At the end of October each year it holds a week-long stargazing festival at various locations including the North Pennines Observatory at Allenheads Ⓕ.

While some come to the North Pennines to look up at the stars, others come here to look deep into the ground. Over many years, geologists have theorised that the North Pennine uplands sit on a mass of granite that rose from the earth's red-hot depths, pushing the overlaying surface rocks higher. The heat of this granite intrusion would have caused veins of minerals like lead, iron, zinc and fluorite to form in the surface rocks – the minerals that brought riches to Pennine mine owners. In 1960 a group of geologists decided to put all this theory to the test by drilling a very deep hole. They chose the old mining village of Rookhope, in the words of W.H. Auden, who was bewitched by the North Pennines, "the most wonderfully desolate of all the dales". At a depth of 390 metres they finally reached the granite they predicted to be present. They stopped when they reached a depth of 800m, finding a temperature of 40°C. The famous borehole, now capped, can still be found across the river from the Rookhope Inn ⓖ (OS grid ref. NY93744278). From here it's a short ride back to Stanhope with more views across Weardale.

PUBS & PIT STOPS

VISITOR CENTRE, Bowlees DL12 0XE (01833 622145) Café in old chapel, waterfalls behind.

LANGDON BECK HOTEL, Forest-in-Teesdale DL12 0XP (01833 622267) Remote hotel and bar in upper Teesdale.

YHA Langdon Beck DL12 0XN (0345 371 9027) Small rural hostel, great views.

GEORGE & DRAGON, Garrigill CA9 3DS (01434 382691) Just off-route, outstanding 17th-century Pennine pub. Good beer, hearty food. Basic rooms.

EASTVIEW B&B, Garrigill CA9 3DU (01434 381561) Pretty stone cottage B&B.

In Nenthead: **MINERS ARMS** (CA9 3PF, Tel: 01434 381 427) pub with B&B; **PLUMBUMS CAFÉ** (01434 408040) in the fabulous Arts and Visitor Centre; **MILL COTTAGE** bunkhouse sleeps up to six (CA9 8PD, 01434 381674).

THE HEMMEL CAFÉ, Allenheads NE47 9HJ (01434 685568) Small café with great Sunday lunches (booking advised).

ALLENHEADS INN, Allenheads NE47 9HJ (01434 685200) Pub with rooms, cycling-friendly, beer from the brilliant Allendale Brewery nearby.

THORN GREEN BUNKHOUSE, Allenheads NE47 9JQ (01434 685234) Bunkhouse and rustic campsite. Breakfast served.

ROOKHOPE INN, Rookhope DL13 2BG (01388 517215) Unpretentious country pub with rooms.

BLACK BULL INN, Frosterley DL13 2SL (01388 527784) Rustic pub 3 miles east of Stanhope but well worth a detour. Excellent food.

BIKE SHOP: North Pennine Cycles, Nenthead CA9 3PF (01434 381324) Small bike workshop, mobile service available.

700m

80km

Great Southern Drove Road

Rookhope mines

Low Force

Nenthead lead works

OVER THE WALL

From the Tyne Valley over to Redesdale and the wild lands of the border reivers

———

At a shade over a metric century (100km) this is a long ride with a few stiff climbs. It is likely to be a long day out on the bike for most people, especially as there's so much to see along the way. Though it can be ridden in one go, it's also a connecting route from railway stations in the Tyne Valley to the villages of Bellingham and Elsdon, which are good bases for Rides No. 10 and 11 that probe even deeper into the Northumberland interior.

In 2005, Hexham was declared Britain's best market town by *Country Life* magazine. The town has been dining off the accolade ever since. It's not an unreasonable claim. Hexham has a well-supported farmers' market, plenty of independent shops, a happening arts scene and some very tasty stone architecture. Then again, Corbridge, Hexham's smaller neighbour, might claim to be even more perfectly formed. Wherever you start, the route heads west up the Tyne past the point where the river divides into its north and south tributaries, and loosely follows the North Tyne Valley upstream to Bellingham.

The south-facing slopes of the Tyne Valley are as sunny as it gets in these northern climes and the whole area is dotted with large country estates. No doubt the Romans found it equally appealing and this may be why they built their wall just to the north. Geology gave them a helping hand

thanks to a natural north-facing rampart formed by an outcrop of hard volcanic rock known as the Whin Sill. Where the North Tyne forced its way through, the Romans built a bridge and fort they named Cilurnum. English Heritage maintains them both: the fort as a visitor attraction and museum (Ⓐ £), while the remains of the bridge are free to visit – just follow the footpath on the right of the road immediately after crossing the present bridge at Chollerford.

Fewer than 30 people now live in Chollerton, the next village, down from over 5,000 in 1851. The stone 'hearse house' in front of the church contains a little museum that gives a flavour of life here in busier times Ⓑ. Inside the church are four large Roman columns, and assorted other Roman artefacts, presumably scavenged and recycled from nearby forts. The next few miles through Barrasford, Birtley and Redesmouth is a joyful roller coaster of lost lanes through woods, fields and open land. Bellingham is an attractive village with a small local history museum that tells the story of the border reivers, the railway that once came here, and much else besides.

Pressing on up the River Rede beyond Bellingham, the landscape is wilder and the skies even bigger. Elsdon is the old capital of Redesdale. 18th-century stone cottages line a large triangular village

START & FINISH: Hexham or Corbridge • DISTANCE: 64 miles / 103km • TOTAL ASCENT: 1115m
TERRAIN: Mostly lanes, one short section of unsurfaced cycleway. Challenging.

Cambo

Wallington

green that slopes from a fortified tower house, where the parish's vicars used to live, to the pinfold, where stray animals were rounded up. A peaceful place today, Elsdon saw much blood and gore over the centuries of Anglo-Scottish confrontations and raids by the clans of border reivers. A mass grave in the churchyard contains over a thousand bodies, possibly the dead from the Battle of Otterburn in 1388, where the Scots routed English forces. Inside the church are marks on the stone pillars where villagers sharpened their swords and arrows. Overlooking the green is the Impromptu Cyclist Café, an institution among cyclists of the north-east; Marion and Allan have been welcoming hungry cyclists since 1978 with steaming cups of tea, beans on toast and their own 'Gibbet Cake'.

The cake takes its name from Winter's Gibbet, the local landmark at the top of a stiff climb east

out of Elsdon ©. Here, in 1792, the rotting corpse of William Winter was hanged after he had been executed for murdering and robbing a local woman. The story goes that he was only caught because the tread of his hobnail boots matched marks at the crime scene. The climb was used in the National Hill Climb Championship in 2004. From the top an exceptionally straight drove road continues east to Gallows Hill. From here the return journey south to the Tyne Valley begins.

Along the way is Wallington Hall ⓓ (NT, £), formerly the home of the Trevelyans, a left-leaning political dynasty of the 19th and early 20th centuries. Just before the big house is the estate village of Cambo where the great landscape gardener Lancelot 'Capability' Brown went to school. His parents worked at nearby Kirkharle Hall where there's now a small exhibition about his life Ⓔ. The highlight of Wallington is its walled garden, complete with glasshouses and a classic 'hot border'. These are accessible by bicycle on a gravel track on the other side of the road from the main entrance to the house.

The next few miles is about picking a way south past fields of wheat and barley to the pretty village of Matfen, recrossing the line of the Roman wall and descending back to the Tyne. Just before crossing the A69 it's worth stopping at the remains of Walker's Pottery to marvel at a pair of gigantic bottle kilns Ⓕ. Once commonplace, there are only 44 left nationwide, most of them in Staffordshire, so these are rare outliers this far north.

Once down in Corbridge head for the 14th-century pele tower – a characteristic defensive fortification of the Anglo-Scottish border – which now houses a microbrewery and pub. The route back to Hexham (if that's where you started) passes what remains of Corbridge Roman town Ⓖ (EH, £). Opposite Hexham's vast chipboard plant is Fentimans, who have been brewing ginger beer and other botanical beverages in the north-east since 1905.

PUBS & PIT STOPS

BARRASFORD ARMS, Barrasford NE48 4AA (01434 681237) Country pub with rooms, good locally sourced food.

Plenty of choice in Bellingham: **CARRIAGES TEA ROOM** (NE48 2DG, 01434 221151) in an old railway carriage; several pubs, a Co-op, a butcher and a bakery. **DEMESNE FARM** (NE48 2BS, 01434 220258) is a perfect campsite and bunkhouse right in the village centre.

RAVENSCLEUGH, near Elsdon NE19 1BW (01830 520896) Farm B&B with camping and swimming lake.

IMPROMPTU CAFÉ, Elsdon NE19 1AA (01830 520389) A landmark among cyclists serving hot drinks, beans on toast, and so on.

BIRD IN BUSH, Elsdon NE19 1AA (01830 520804) Unspoilt village pub. Quality local food, own microbrewery. Three bedrooms and a bunkhouse.

COFFEE HOUSE, Kirkharle Courtyard NE19 2PE (01830 540362) Light lunches and cream teas near Capability Brown's childhood home.

CAPHEATON TEA ROOM, Silver Hill, Capheaton NE19 2AA. Just off route, a cyclists' favourite in an old tin shack. Open most weekends except deepest winter.

MATFEN VILLAGE STORE, NE20 0RL (01661 886202) Village shop and café serving good, simple home-cooked food.

THE PELE, Market Place, Corbridge NE45 5AW (07565 801463) Micropub in medieval stone tower.

HEXHAM TOWN B&B, Hexham NE46 2HA (07714 292602) Stylish, good-value B&B.

BOUCHON BISTRO, Hexham NE46 3NJ (01434 609 943) Classic French cooking.

BIKE HIRE: Eco Cycle Adventures, Hexham NE46 3PU (01434 610076) Hybrids, MTBs and e-bikes for hire.

400m

110km

Walker's Pottery

Elsdon

Impromtu Café, Elsdon

NORTHERN EXPOSURE

A ride to the Scottish border past the meadows of Coquetdale
and the bleak hills of the Otterburn firing range

———

This ride is a natural extension to Ride No. 9, going deep into the Cheviot Hills to within sight of the Scottish border. It's a ride of two halves; the second half, across the wild, windblown moors of the Otterburn military training area, is only open on days when the army is not training. Dates are published online. Even if the range is closed to the public, the first half makes for a lovely out-and-back route, but I would suggest waiting for a weekend when the range is fully open to get the most out of this ride.

The ride starts in Elsdon, where old stone houses surround a village green spread out like a giant picnic rug beneath a parish church known as the cathedral of Redesdale. Start or end at the brilliant 'Impromptu Cyclist Café' at the top of the green which has been a landmark for local cyclists for over 40 years. The walls are filled with photographs and artefacts that document decades of racing, touring and recreational cycling in the north east and beyond.

The first task is to cross from Redesdale into Coquetdale, following Sustrans Route 68, the Pennine Cycleway, a 350-mile-long route from Derby to Berwick-upon-Tweed. It's a stiff climb but a long, gentle and scenic descent alongside the Grasslees Burn, which flows into the River Coquet. The next twenty miles, climbing gradually along Upper Coquetdale, is up there among the best cycling anywhere in Britain. The Coquet is a constant companion, and changes in character from lazy meander across a broad flood plain to flashing stream tumbling down deep ravines.

Unless it's blowing a gale, Coquetdale feels so very tranquil. Yet it was not always so. For centuries there was a simmering conflict between Scotland and England, and regular armed skirmishes. Life was hard and people joined together in kinship clans to defend themselves, but also to conduct raids across the border. They became known as 'reivers', a word derived from the Old English *rēafian*, meaning to rob, plunder or pillage. Murder, rape, kidnap, extortion, theft, arson and revenge were an inescapable part of life here. Overlooking a broad, meandering section of the river are the remains of Woodhouses Bastle, a fortified farmhouse dating from 1602 (access via a short footpath from the road) Ⓐ.

The era of the reivers came to an end in the 1700s but the borderland's reputation for law-lessness persisted with the smuggling and illicit distillation of whisky. There were small, illegal distilleries all over the valley. Liquor was bought and sold under cryptic and evocative names like 'new milk', 'knives and forks' and 'grey hens'. But the main business was always farming. Essential

---

START & FINISH: Elsdon • DISTANCE: 39 miles / 63km • TOTAL ASCENT: 934m
TERRAIN: Lanes. Check military firing times. Moderate.

Woodhouses Bastle

Otterburn Ranges

Star Inn, Harbottle

to traditional upland farming were hay meadows. Once a common sight, agricultural intensification means there are less than three thousand acres left across the whole of Britain. They are one of our lost landscapes and a precious haven for rare plants, insects and birds. A few still cling on here in Coquetdale, and are rightly cherished. The best time to visit is early July, just before the hay is cut and stored for a winter that's long and can get bitterly cold. A good spot is around Barrowburn Ⓒ.

At Harbottle, the remnants of a Norman castle overlook the valley. The castle was repeatedly attacked and besieged by the Scots and abandoned once and for all in the 17th century with much of the masonry used for other buildings in the village. Alwinton is a meeting of the ways and must have

been a much busier place than it is now, especially when the drovers were passing through. On the second Saturday in October the village plays host to a Border Shepherds Show, the last agricultural show of the borders area before winter sets in.

Beyond Shillmoor the valley narrows and the road runs beside the river. There are some good wild swim spots with small cascades and plunge pools Ⓑ. The water is straight off the mountain – dark, peaty and bracing, so best saved for a really hot day. The valley winds its way up and up, getting narrower with every turn. The real climbing begins just past Fulhope. From here it all starts to feel very wild, especially in the prevailing westerly wind.

At Chew Green, right on the border with Scotland, are the remains of Roman military camps overlaid by the remains of medieval settlements ⓓ. The best view of the site is from above. That's where the road now goes, heading straight uphill on the course of Dere Street, the main Roman road into Scotland which connected York with the Antonine Wall at the Firth of Forth and in use by armies, traders, pilgrims, travellers and drovers ever since.

The route now enters the Otterburn military firing ranges. The tarmac is well maintained and it's great riding on the bleak moorland plateau that is such a contrast to pretty Coquetdale. The army has been here since 1911 and archaeologists have recently discovered trenches used for training troops during the First World War. It's the UK's largest firing range and used for training using artillery and rockets. If the red flags are flying, keep out. The route makes the most of the military roads but on days when they are closed you can almost always turn right at Cottonshope Head ⓔ and follow the road down to Cottonshopeburnfoot and take the A68 back to Elsdon. Though not especially busy, it is a fast, straight main road and far from a lost lane.

PUBS & PIT STOPS

RAVENSCLEUGH, near Elsdon NE19 1BW (01830 520896) Lovely farm B&B with basic camping and wild swimming lake.

IMPROMPTU CAFÉ, Elsdon NE19 1AA (01830 520389) A landmark among cyclists serving hot drinks, beans on toast, and so on.

BIRD IN BUSH, Elsdon NE19 1AA (01830 520804) Unspoilt village pub. Quality local food, own microbrewery. Three bedrooms and a bunkhouse.

THE STAR INN, Netherton NE65 7HD (01669 630238) Off-route but worth a visit for fans of historic pub interiors. Very limited hours.

THE STAR INN, Harbottle NE65 7DG (01669 650221) Old school village pub.

CLENNELL HALL, Harbottle NE65 7BG (01669 650377) Rambling country house with rooms, bunk rooms and camping.

ROSE AND THISTLE, Alwinton NE65 7BQ (01669 650226) Tardis like pub, sunny garden. Pub grub. It's said Walter Scott stayed here researching Rob Roy.

BARROWBURN FARM, Barrowburn NE65 7BP (01669 650059) Remote camping barn and basic campsite surrounded by meadows.

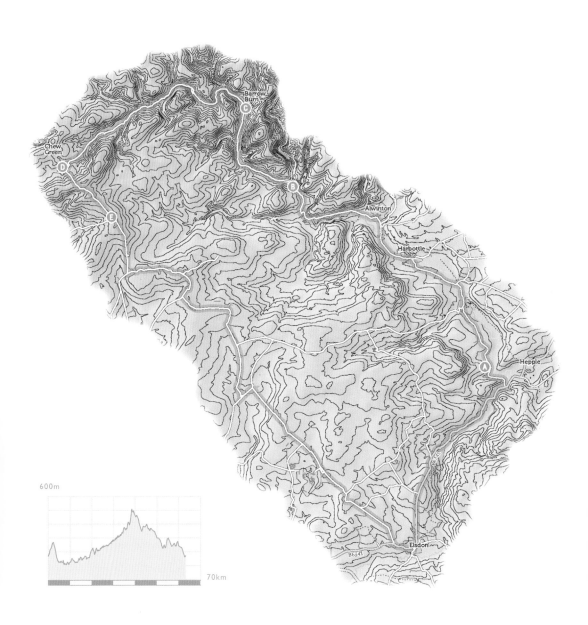

600m

70km

Coquetdale

INTO THE WILD

A gravel road adventure from the pleasant pastures of the
North Tyne into the rugged expanses of the Kielder Forest

———

Bellingham makes a perfect base for exploring Northumberland's wild and sparsely populated interior. The town, whose name is pronounced locally with a soft g as in 'fringe', sits on Sustrans's long-distance Reivers coast-to-coast routes (there's a road version and an off-road version) and the even longer Pennine Cycleway. It has a co-op, three pubs, a butcher, a baker, a bookshop, a tea room in an old railway carriage, a small museum of local life and history, and the most perfect farm campsite and bunkhouse right in the heart of town.

The town sits beside the River North Tyne, and this ride follows it upstream to Kielder Water, where the river is confined in the largest man-made lake in Britain before striking out on gravel tracks across the vast conifer plantation of the Kielder Forest. It's easy, gently undulating riding on a quiet lane that criss-crosses the route of the old railway line. The village of Falstone sits just beneath the Kielder Dam. If, for any reason, the dam failed, the village would be washed away in an instant. Since 1885 Falstone has hosted an annual Border Shepherds Show. It's usually in the last week of August and there are sheepdog trials, a livestock show, a cake show, a fell race, and plenty of beer drinking. The route follows the old railway line trackbed up to the top of the dam, at which point you can look out beyond the reservoir-brutalist

valve tower and get a sense of the sheer immensity of Kielder Water. Built in the 1970s to supply water to the industrial north-east, it contains 200 billion litres of water. That's enough to give every person on the planet a three-minute shower. The water level is kept topped up across a huge and rain-sodden catchment area that extends to the Scottish border. Kielder Water is one big reason gardeners in the North East rarely, if ever, have to worry about hosepipe bans.

Northumbrian Water, which runs the reservoir, has done a brilliant job of promoting it for leisure and recreation by creating walking and cycling paths and giving people more to look at than just water and trees. The Lakeside Way is a 26-mile-long walking and cycling path around the lake and there are several large-scale art installations to see along the way. In summer, ferries take passengers across the water. A road runs along the southern side, and this is an option if your time is tight. But you would miss out on the pleasure of a wilder, traffic-free way along the northern shore. As there is no road access, it's quieter here, yet there is more art to see. My top three are the Wave Chamber, a womb-like stone cairn into which the light and sound of the lake are projected, to truly mesmerising effect Ⓐ; the large, rotating Janus Chairs Ⓑ; and Silvas Capitalis, an exquisitely carved, giant wooden head that you can

---

START & FINISH: Bellingham • DISTANCE: 47 miles / 75km • TOTAL ASCENT: 1054m
TERRAIN: Lanes and some extended sections of good gravel tracks. Challenging.

Lakeside Trail, Kielder Water

climb inside ⓒ. This is public art at its best. The path is surprisingly hilly for a lakeside route but the surface is good, fine-packed gravel. It's perfect for young teenagers to expend some energy without having to worry about traffic.

At Kielder Castle there's a visitor centre, a café, a bike hire centre and a campsite ⓓ. There is also a futuristic maze made from stone gabions to get lost in. From here the route heads uphill on Forest Drive. It's a toll road (bicycles go free) and is unsurfaced for most of its length so there's next to no motor traffic. The col at the top of the climb is Blakehope Nick at 457m above sea level ⓔ. Marking the spot is The Nick, another amazing art installation. It is a pentagonal timber shelter-sculpture built by students from Newcastle University's School of Architecture, Planning and Landscape.

It's all downhill to Redesdale and the hamlet of Blakehopeburnhaugh – a compound name that claims to be the second-longest place name in England, only beaten by Cottonshopeburnfoot a mile to the north. If the visual diet of gravel, water, pine and moor has proven a little monotonous, then you can revive your eyes by taking a short detour on foot on a 1¼-mile woodland walk to the Hindhope Linn waterfall (it's signed from the track just south of Blakehopeburnhaugh) ⓕ.

The route continues along a gravel track south, through more dark and spooky conifer plantations including a section that has recently been clear-felled. The expanse of splintered stumps and ripped and tangled undergrowth has the atmosphere of a war zone fallen silent after the combatants have fled the scene. Eventually, the forest gives way to the open moor where you'll meet nobody but sheep and the occasional lonely shepherd. After one last short section of gravel it's on to the B6320 for the descent back to Bellingham.

PUBS & PIT STOPS

Plenty of choice in Bellingham: **CARRIAGES TEA ROOM** (NE48 2DG, 01434 221151) in an old railway carriage; several pubs, a Co-op, a butcher and a bakery. **DEMESNE FARM** (NE48 2BS, 01434 220258) is a perfect campsite and bunkhouse right in the village centre.

THE BOE RIGG, Charlton NE48 1PE (01434 240663) Just off-route, B&B, bistro and back-to-basics campsite.

HESLEYSIDE HUTS, near Bellingham NE48 2LA (01434 220068) Luxurious shepherds' huts on a country estate beside the North Tyne River.

BLACKCOCK INN, Falstone NE48 1AA (01434 240200) Stone-built pub with reasonably priced rooms. Pub grub.

OLD SCHOOL TEAROOM, Falstone NE48 1AA (01434 240459) No-frills tea room in a Victorian schoolhouse.

THE PHEASANT INN, Stannersburn NE48 1DD (01434 240382) Just off-route, but the best pub in the area. Great food. Rooms.

KIELDER CASTLE CAFÉ, Kielder Village NE48 1ER (01434 250100) Light lunches and snacks.

KIELDER VILLAGE CAMPSITE, Kielder Village NE48 1EJ (01434 239257) Large campsite with glamping pods.

BIKE SHOP: The Bike Place, Kielder Village NE48 1ER (01434 250457) Bike shop with full range of bikes and e-bikes to hire.

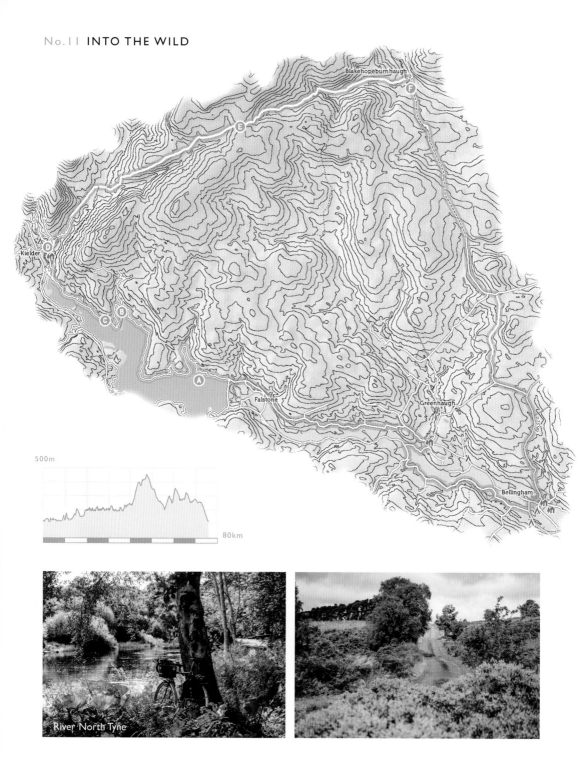

500m

80km

River North Tyne

THE OLD NORTH

A linear route taking in the ancient castles, huge beaches
and tiny harbours of the Northumberland coast

———

The Northumberland coast has three qualities that make it uniquely well suited to cycling. It's beautiful, the coast roads are quiet, and there are no hills. No wonder that National Cycle Route 1 runs all the way from Newcastle upon Tyne north to Berwick-upon-Tweed. It's a great route and this northern half, which is the wildest and most scenic, is do-able in a day with a train back. A weekend would allow for any detours and a proper look around the ruined castles and the Holy Island of Lindisfarne, and the odd swim in the sea. The route can be done in either direction, but if you plan to visit Lindisfarne island, it's essential to check ahead for the tide times as the causeway is only passable for three to four hours each side of low tide. The prevailing wind is from the south-west, so it makes sense to ride south to north. Then again, there can be strong northerlies, too.

Alnmouth grew up as a port with a fishing fleet, shipyards and a trade exporting grain and other produce from the Northumberland interior. Shifting sands and the coming of the railways hurt the port, though the railways also brought holidaymakers, and the village grew into a coastal resort with one of the oldest – and most scenic – golf courses in England. It retains its well-heeled charm. A short way up the coastal lane is Boulmer (pronounced 'Boomer'), an unassum-ing fishing village that was once the smuggling capital of Northumberland, with the nefarious activities centred on the Fishing Boat Inn. North of Boulmer there's a short off-road section via a pair of tiny sandy coves, both good for a swim Ⓐ. If you're on a road bike you may prefer the road via Longhoughton. The next village is Craster, with its tight harbour and a smokehouse famous for its kippers. On the headland north of Craster are the ruins of Dunstanburgh Castle Ⓑ. They're only accessible on foot, and there's a stile to cross on the north side. Beyond the castle the sands of Embleton Bay stretch into the distance. At the north end of the bay, and off-route, is Low Newton-by-the-Sea Ⓒ. It is the loveliest beach on the coast with a brilliant pub serving local beer and simple, home-made food. From Embleton the route heads inland for a few miles, skirting the edge of Seahouses, from where you can take a boat trip out to the Farne Islands to see seals, porpoises, puffins, guillemots and many other seabirds.

Unlike ruined Dunstanburgh, the castle at Bamburgh is very much intact Ⓓ. Its stout form, built atop a natural outcrop of volcanic rock, commands the channel between the mainland and the Farne Islands. Few places in Britain are quite so steeped in history. The present castle is of Norman design but before that it was the seat

---

START: Alnmouth • FINISH: Berwick-upon-Tweed • DISTANCE: 57 miles / 91km • TOTAL ASCENT: 550m
TERRAIN: Lanes and a few off-road sections which can be muddy when wet. Train return. Moderate.

Holy Island causeway

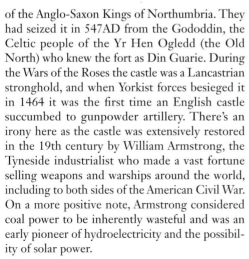

of the Anglo-Saxon Kings of Northumbria. They had seized it in 547AD from the Gododdin, the Celtic people of the Yr Hen Ogledd (the Old North) who knew the fort as Din Guarie. During the Wars of the Roses the castle was a Lancastrian stronghold, and when Yorkist forces besieged it in 1464 it was the first time an English castle succumbed to gunpowder artillery. There's an irony here as the castle was extensively restored in the 19th century by William Armstrong, the Tyneside industrialist who made a vast fortune selling weapons and warships around the world, including to both sides of the American Civil War. On a more positive note, Armstrong considered coal power to be inherently wasteful and was an early pioneer of hydroelectricity and the possibility of solar power.

North of Bamburgh there's a nice rough stuff option along the coast road via Blackrocks Point lighthouse Ⓔ. From the sandy expanse of Budle Bay the route heads inland until it reaches the causeway road to Lindisfarne Ⓕ. The causeway is under water for several hours around high tide – so if you venture across be sure to check the tide times and don't get stranded. Omitting Holy Island shortens the ride by 8 miles but if you have time, and the tides are favourable, it's worth getting across. The island was the base for the Celtic monks who converted Northern England to Christianity and who produced the dazzlingly illuminated Lindisfarne Gospels which are now in the possession of the British Library in London. The island is mostly car-free and it's a pleasure to explore, from the castle, ruined abbey and harbour on the south, to the little-known sandy swimming beach at Coves Haven on the north coast .

North of Lindisfarne it's mostly salt marshes and dunes, and the route follows NCR 1 on a range of surfaces ranging from tarmac to hard-packed gravel before a final section along the cliffs which can be hard-going in the wet. This is one of Britain's great coastal bike routes, and the way it's been neglected by the powers-that-be is a real shame. With a better surface many more people would be able to enjoy it. Like Carlisle on the east coast, Berwick-upon-Tweed has its own border town vibe, and there are some good pubs to while away the time before the train back to Alnmouth.

PUBS & PIT STOPS

THE RED LION, Alnmouth NE66 2RJ (01665 830584) Coaching inn with comfortable rooms.

SCOTTS OF ALNMOUTH, Alnmouth NE66 2RS. Deli with all the fixings for a gourmet picnic. Excellent pies.

JOLLY FISHERMAN, Craster NE66 3TR (01665 576461) Well-cellared beers and local seafood. Booking advised.

CRASTER SEAFOOD RESTAURANT, Craster NE66 3TR (01665 576230) Seafood café beside Robson's smokehouse (which has a takeaway counter). Booking advised in summer.

PIPERS PITCH, Craster NE66 3TW (07585 605607) Shack in the Craster quarry car park serving tasty, fishy bites and its famous haggis in a bap.

GREYS INN, Embleton NE66 3UZ (01665 576983) Good selection of ales, standard pub grub.

JOINERS ARMS, High Newton NE66 3EA (01665 576112) Swanky gastropub with rooms. Booking advised.

SHIP INN, Low Newton-by-the-Sea NE66 3EL (01665 576262) Fisherman's pub by the beach. Simple home-cooked food. Worth the detour.

In Seahouses, **SWALLOW FISH** (NE68 7RB, 01665 721052) has been smoking herrings since 1843, while **YE OLDE SHIP INN** (NE68 7RD, 01665 720200) is a salty seafarers' pub.

Several run-of-the mill cafés in Bamburgh but good picnic materials from **R CARTER & SON** and **THE PANTRY,** both on Front Street.

THE BARN AT BEAL, Beal TD15 2PB (01289 540044) Bustling café and campsite on a farm overlooking Holy Island.

PILGRIMS COFFEE HOUSE, Holy Island TD15 2SJ (01289 389109) The best coffee for miles around.

In Berwick-upon-Tweed head for groovy Bridge Street. **BARRELS ALE HOUSE** (TD15 1ES, 01289 308013) is full of character while the **CURFEW** micropub (TD15 1AQ, 07842 912268) sells craft ales and pies and the **MULE ON ROUGE** café (TD15 1ES) has good, vege-friendly food. Uptown on Church Street is the **CORNER HOUSE CAFÉ** (TD15 1EE, 01289 304748) to relax in a big leather sofa by the open fire.

BIKE SHOP: The Bike Shop, Alnwick NE66 2PF (07599 350000) Bike shop and hire, delivery and collection service available.

Budle Bay

200m

100km

Bamburgh

Holy Island

Belford

Fenwick

Spittal

Scremerston

Berwick upon Tweed

East Ord

Ship Inn, Low Newton

Craster

Dunstanburgh Castle

NORTH
YORK MOORS &
YORKSHIRE
WOLDS

PURPLE HAZE

An adventurous and largely traffic-free ride taking in forest, moor and coast

———

There aren't a whole lot of roads in the eastern half of the North York Moors, and to get the most out of the landscape you have to venture onto its unsurfaced tracks and trails. This circuit pairs a fantastic gravel track across the moors with a section of the Cinder Track along the old coastal railway line between Scarborough and Whitby.

The ride begins in Whitby, a seaside town that has it all: a sandy beach, steep streets leading down to a busy harbour, ornate Victorian architecture, and lots of independent shops and cafés. Looming above it all are the dark ruins of Whitby Abbey. No wonder Bram Stoker chose it as the setting for his best passage in *Dracula*. Drawing on newspaper accounts of a real Whitby shipwreck, Stoker describes how a Russian schooner races into the harbour driven by the waves of a powerful storm. The ship's captain is dead and his body is lashed to the helm. As the ship crashes into the pier, a huge wild dog springs from the hold, leaps ashore, bounds up the steps leading to the abbey and disappears into the night. *Dracula* has arrived. Whitby loves its *Dracula* connection and since 1994 the town has hosted the Whitby Goth Weekend, a twice-yearly gathering where the town is overrun by serious-looking folk wearing velvet cloaks, leather and lace, dark eyeliner and back-combed hair.

The ride starts out on the Cinder Track, heading across a viaduct over the River Esk, and at Stainsacre takes to country roads that climb up into the high moor. At May Beck the tarmac ends and the gravel begins. It's a steady climb to the high point of the ride at Stony Leas Ⓐ. Here, from August to October the flowering heather turns the drab moorland a psychedelic purple. A 10th-century stone cross marks the crossing point of two ancient trackways across the moors, and the junction of four medieval parishes. A more recent landmark is the radar pyramid at RAF Fylingdales, away to the west. The top-secret installation was built during the Cold War as part of the system that would give the infamous four-minute warning of an imminent nuclear attack. It also tracks objects orbiting in space and keeps tabs on foreign spy satellites flying over the UK.

Descending from the open moor, it's back into the forest for the winding descent to the hamlet of Langdale End and the Moorcock Inn, a time-warp of a country pub with limited opening hours Ⓑ. Two miles off-route to the west is the Dalby Forest and its dense network of mountain bike tracks which offer something for everyone, from gentle family routes through to the black route used for the World Cup in 2010.

START & FINISH: Whitby • DISTANCE: 40 miles / 65km • TOTAL ASCENT: 987m
TERRAIN: Mostly good forest tracks and unsurfaced railway trail, a few connecting lanes. Moderate.

The Moorcock Inn

Lilla Cross

From Hackness the road heads uphill again through the hamlet of Silpho. It was near here in 1957 that three local men driving across the moor saw a glowing object in the sky. It suddenly fell to the ground and they went to investigate. The small metal disc was about 40cm across and covered with strange hieroglyphics, not unlike the flying saucer found at Roswell in the United States. The Silpho mystery object turned out to be an elaborate hoax but not before it had fooled many, including a former head of the RAF who examined it. What was definitely not a hoax was the discovery in 1989 of a cache of arms including Semtex, a high explosive used by the IRA, in approximately the same location. It was found shortly before the Conservative Party conference just down the coast in Scarborough and sparked a major security alert.

A short section of off-road track connects to more lanes through moor and fields until eventually you'll see the sea. From the top of Stoupe Brow © you get a big view of the coast, from Ravenscar to the headland beyond Robin Hood's Bay. From here the route picks up the Cinder Track. Once the railway route between Whitby and Scarborough, the trail could be one of the glories of traffic-free cycling in Britain but is let down by poor maintenance and a second-rate surface that gets muddy after rain. The good news is that plans are afoot to upgrade it. Maybe Cinderella shall go to the ball after all.

Robin Hood's Bay is a little fishing village with a sideline of smuggling that has long since transitioned into tourism. Even so, with old buildings stacked up along an absurdly steep road that discourages access by car, it retains an indisputable charm. At low tide the beach is a good spot for rock-pooling and fossil hunting. Robin Hood's Bay is the end point of the Coast to Coast walk from St Bees in West Cumbria, an unofficial and mostly unsigned long-distance walking route designed by Alfred Wainwright who envisaged it as a twelve-day journey.

If the climb back up from the beach is a struggle, then spare a thought for the lifeboat crew who, during a ferocious winter storm in 1881, came to the aid of a ship that had run aground in the bay. Unable to launch the lifeboat in Whitby, they pulled it six miles overland using eighteen horses, with scores of people frantically clearing away snowdrifts that blocked their path. Astonishingly, the journey took just two hours and all six stricken sailors were saved.

On the way into Whitby the route passes the ruined abbey and St Mary's church overlooking the harbour ⓓ. You can either walk down the steep cobbles beside the famous 199 church steps or roll down the road.

PUBS & PIT STOPS

THE MOORCOCK INN, Langdale End YO13 0BN (01723 882268) Time warp of a rural pub with limited opening hours, so call ahead. Bar meals served.

THE FALCON INN, Harwood Dale YO13 0DY (01723 870717) Large roadhouse pub with camping pods.

Plenty of options in Robin Hood's Bay. THE LAUREL INN (YO22 4SE, 01947 880400) is a tiny pub with plenty of old-world charm, and the BAY HOTEL (YO22 4SJ, 01947 880278) is a walkers' favourite. COVE CAFÉ (YO22 4SQ, 01947 880180) has a terrace with good views. For fish and chips, FISH BOX (YO22 4SE, 01947 880595) has lots of seating, while MARIONDALE FISHERIES (YO22 4SW, 01947 880426) is down by the quayside.

HARE & HOUNDS, Hawsker YO22 4LH (01947 880 453) Popular gastropub between Robin Hood's Bay and Whitby. Food served all day Fri-Sun.

RUSWARP HALL, Ruswarp YO21 1NH (01947 602801) Lovely Jacobean country house hotel. Reasonably priced rooms.

WHITBY BREWERY, East Cliff, Whitby YO22 4JR (01947 228871) Brewery tap by the ruins of Whitby Abbey.

Plenty of choice in Whitby: THE BLACK HORSE INN (YO22 4BH, 01947 602906) is an old town landmark serving cask ales and 'Yorkshire tapas'; great fish and chips at TRENCHERS (YO21 1DH, 01947 603212) and the historic MAGPIE CAFÉ (YO21 3PU, 01947 602058). BOTHAM'S on Skinner Street (YO21 3AH) for old-school baked goods and the WHITBY DELI on Flowergate (YO21 3BA) for more modern fare.

BIKE HIRE: Trailways Cycle Hire, Hawsker YO22 4LB (01947 820207) Cycle hire on the Cinder Track near Whitby.

Whitby

Whitby Abbey

Robin Hood's Bay

AWHEEL IN WHEELDALE

Up from verdant Eskdale into the open country of
the high moors and back along an ancient way

The River Esk marks the northern edge of the North York Moors. It's a lush, steep-sided valley fed by becks that tumble down from the moors on either side, carving deep gorges as they go. Somehow, Victorian railway engineers managed to squeeze a railway line along the valley floor, and even more miraculously, it survived the brutal cuts to Britain's railway network in the 1960s. But there's no room for a road, or even a footpath. This makes the valley challenging terrain for human-powered transport. It feels as though the lanes cross every contour line on the map and go every which way but straight. If they're not going up, they're going down, usually at double-figure gradients. After an hour's riding in the Esk Valley it feels like a relief to be on the long, straight roads atop the finger-like ridges of the high moor.

The ride starts in the village of Grosmont (pronounced with a silent s). The village has two railways: the Esk Valley line from Middlesbrough to Whitby, and George Stephenson's line across the moors to Pickering, now run as a heritage railway. The old-fashioned level crossing and the to-ing and fro-ing of steam locos lend the village the atmosphere of bygone times, and it is a good base for exploring the area. Heading west along the river, a gravel track to Egton Bridge dodges one big hill but soon enough the climbing begins,

first on the north side of the valley then up the south side through the village of Glaisdale and up Glaisdale Rigg onto the moorland plateau.

The moors were once dotted with quarries and mines but today the biggest business is grouse shooting. This involves a line of 'beaters' blowing whistles and waving flags to chase wild red grouse towards a line of men with guns (and it is almost always men) who are waiting to shoot them as they fly past. Lines of shooting butts – sometimes made of wood, sometimes from stone – are visible from the road. When not in use the more spacious ones can make for handy shelters for a brew-up or a bivvy. The landscape of the moors is managed to maximise grouse numbers. Boggy areas are drained, and strips of heather are periodically burned to provide the food and the low-level cover that grouse prefer. Environmentalists argue this creates a 'grouse monoculture' which increases the risk of wildfires and flooding in valleys, increases carbon emissions and reduces the overall ecological variety of the uplands. Wild animals that threaten grouse – foxes, stoats, hares and crows – are trapped or shot. The hen harrier, a bird of prey that was once widespread in Britain, is close to eradication from the uplands. The big estates challenge all this, arguing that a managed, heather-rich moor that's good for grouse is also

---

START & FINISH: Grosmont • DISTANCE: 34 miles / 55km • TOTAL ASCENT: 972m
TERRAIN: All lanes. Moderate.

Beggar's Bridge

good for other ground-nesting birds like golden plover, curlew and lapwing. They say that the persecution of hen harriers is the work of a small minority of renegade gamekeepers, and modern moorland management is much more ecologically aware. People pay thousands of pounds for a single day's shooting (£75 a grouse is a going rate) and much of this money trickles down into the local economy and local employment. It's a debate that will run and run.

The moorland plateau comes to an abrupt end above Rosedale. It's hard to imagine, but from the 1850s to the 1920s a huge iron ore industry grew up here, after the discovery of an abundance of high-grade magnetic ores. The population grew from 558 to nearly 3,000. A railway served the mines and is now a nine-mile walking and off-road cycling route that passes many of the abandoned industrial buildings scattered across the valley. It's a really rewarding detour if you have time and don't mind a bit of gravel riding Ⓐ.

The descent into Rosedale Abbey is pretty steep but the climb on the far side of the valley is insane. With an average gradient of 13% and a maximum of 33%, Chimney Bank shares the title of steepest road in England with the Hardknott Pass in Cumbria, earning its reputation as a chain breaker.

Ignoring the siren call of Chimney Bank, the route follows the valley road down to the Cropton Brewery Ⓑ (tours are available) on the very edge of the Vale of Pickering. It then rounds the site of the Roman camps at Cawthorne which you can ride to, down a track on the left of the lane Ⓒ. All that remains is earthworks covered in heather but the views across the moors are immense.

For the return to Grosmont one option is to ride down to Pickering and hop on a steam train, but to do that would be to miss out on one of the great lost lanes of the North. With the name of Wheeldale Road it sounds to be tailor-made for the touring cyclist, but it's much older than that. There are some remains just off the present route that could be Roman, or an earlier Bronze Age boundary marker, or a medieval trackway . It remains a puzzle. What is incontestable is the solitude and beauty of the road, which fords a couple of streams along the way. It just gets better the further along you go, reaching a climax as the dark outline of Whitby Abbey appears in the distance just before the descent back into the deep green ravine of the Esk Valley.

PUBS & PIT STOPS

POSTGATE INN, Egton Bridge YO21 1UX (01947 895241) Handsome Victorian country pub with B&B.

HORSESHOE HOTEL, Egton Bridge YO21 1XE (01947 895245) Small country house hotel, good value. Sunday lunch recommended.

YORKSHIRE CYCLE HUB, Great Fryup Dale YO21 2AP (01287 669098) A few miles off-route, but a good base for exploring the area. Comfortable bunkhouse, world-class breakfasts. Bike hire available.

GRAZE ON THE GREEN, Rosedale Abbey YO18 8RA (01751 417468) Tea room and café serving full breakfasts and light lunches.

DALE HEAD FARM TEA GARDEN, Rosedale YO18 8RL (01751 417353) Superb tea shop on the optional gravel route up the valley. Shepherd's hut for hire.

NEW INN, Cropton YO18 8HH (01751 417330) Pub with onsite brewery. Rooms and camping available.

CROSSING CLUB, Grosmont YO22 5QE (07766 197744) Meet steam railway volunteers in this friendly micropub. Evenings only.

BIKE HIRE: Yorkshire Cycle Hub, see above.

400m

50km

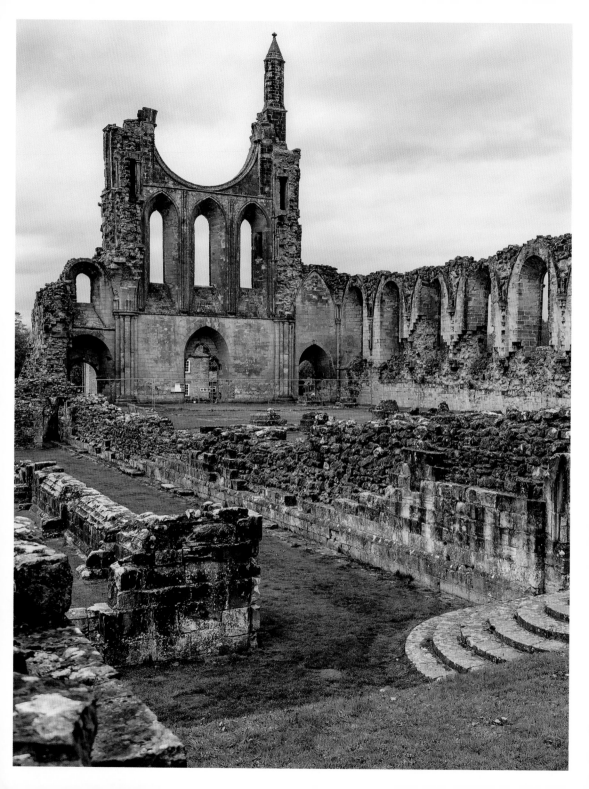

A SENTIMENTAL JOURNEY

A pleasant pootle around the limestone villages, ruined abbeys,
and grand country houses of the Hambleton Hills

The Hambleton Hills are the westernmost outcrop of a band of limestone that forms the southern edge of the North York Moors. They come to an abrupt halt in craggy cliffs overlooking the flood plain of the Vale of Mowbray and across to the high ground of the Yorkshire Dales and the Pennines. As a building material, the limestone, which is the compressed crushed remains of coral that grew in the warm, tropical seas that once covered England, oozes honey-toned loveliness and makes the whole area look more Cotswold than Yorkshire.

The ride begins in Thirsk, a good-looking town with many handsome Georgian buildings, and a fabulous Edwardian cinema. The town's Monday market dates back to 1145 and there's another on Saturdays. In the stagecoach era Thirsk was a stopping point on the York Road (a branch of the Great North Road) which may explain the number of pubs and coaching inns in the market-place. A small but perfectly formed town history museum is housed in the birthplace of Thomas Lord, one of the town's most famous sons. Lord was a professional cricketer and set up the cricket ground in London that continues to bear his name. The museum also tells the moving story of local Quakers who supplied relief to starving German civilians in the aftermath of the First World War. Right opposite the town museum is the much larger World of James Herriot Museum (£) devoted to the Scottish vet who lived here and had a sideline writing semi-autobiographical books about his work. Wildly popular, they were adapted into films and the TV series *All Creatures Great and Small*. No one has done more to fix a a certain idea of the Yorkshire countryside in the popular imagination.

On the way through Bagby, look out for the astonishing front garden of Eric Marshall, a railway enthusiast who has built there a model railway complete with stations, houses, castles, tunnels, a cable car and a windmill. Each piece is handmade by Eric; at Christmas time the whole scene is lit with fairy lights Ⓐ.

The next village is Kilburn, which sits just beneath the wooded crags of Roulston Scar, the location of the biggest Iron Age fort in Northern England and the Kilburn White Horse, one of the few hill figures in the North Ⓑ. Kilburn was also the home of furniture maker Robert Thompson. Working in Yorkshire oak, he was part of a revival of craftsmanship inspired by the Arts and Crafts movement. Thompson signed his work by carving a figure of a mouse, earning him the nickname 'the mouseman of Kilburn'. The workshop is going strong and is open to visitors, and you can find examples of his work in the village church.

START & FINISH: Thirsk • DISTANCE: 44 miles / 71km • TOTAL ASCENT: 803m
TERRAIN: All lanes. Moderate.

Thirsk

Beyond Kilburn is the village of Coxwold, with Shandy Hall, the home of Laurence Sterne, the Irish clergyman and novelist Ⓒ (£). *The Life and Opinions of Tristram Shandy, Gentleman* redefined the possibilities of the novel, while *A Sentimental Journey* ushered in a new age of travel writing with a greater emphasis on personal experience. Not bad for a man who only took up writing full-time at the age of 46 and died of tuberculosis nine years later.

Little remains of magnificent Byland Abbey but you get a sense of the large round window which inspired the Rose Window at York Minster Ⓓ. There some very well-preserved medieval floor tiles that are worth a look. Entry is free.

Nunnington Hall is a big old country house that was renovated in the 1920s by Walter Brierley who, like the mouseman of Kilburn, was a follower of the Arts and Crafts movement.

The house and gardens are now owned by the National Trust Ⓔ (£).

After crossing over the young River Rye, the route turns west for the return to Thirsk, via Helmsley, which acts as the capital of Upper Ryedale. It's got a good castle (£, EH) and a four-acre walled garden with a café in the Victorian vine house.

There's no avoiding the B-road up the hill from Helmsley, which can be busy on summer weekends, but it's not far until the turn to Rievaulx Ⓕ. The landscaped gardens and classically styled temples of Rievaulx Terrace (£, NT) show the influence of the Grand Tour on the imagination of the landed and wealthy of the 18th century. There are views down to the ruins of the Cistercian abbey in the valley below (£, EH). The abbey was one of the richest in England, with 6,000 acres in land used for mining lead and iron, rearing sheep, and trading in wool and cloth. The clever monks were smelting good-quality cast iron using a very early form of blast furnace a few miles upriver at Laskill, centuries before the Industrial Revolution.

From Rievaulx it's back across the River Rye and uphill to the escarpment of the Hambleton Hills. The road along the ridge must have been in use since prehistory and became a key route for drovers bringing cattle from Scotland down to markets at York.

From the top it's a short detour south to Sutton Bank, a place that is often described, with typical Yorkshire modesty, as the "finest view in England" ⑥. Wordsworth came here and composed a sonnet. "Dark and more dark the shades of evening fell", it opens, for they have arrived too late. In the fading light of the "glowing west", he can visualise an "Indian citadel, Temple of Greece, and minster... objects all for the eye of silent rapture". From the ridge the route turns off down Boltby Bank and a joyfully undulating last few miles back to Thirsk.

PUBS & PIT STOPS

In Thirsk you can stock up for a picnic at **JOHNSON'S** butchers (YO7 1PQ) and the **UPSTAIRS DOWNSTAIRS** café, bakery and deli (YO7 1HD).

THE BLACK SWAN, Oldstead YO61 4BL (01347 868387) Michelin-starred restaurant with rooms. Locally grown and foraged foods.

STAR INN, Harome YO62 5JE (01439 770397) High-end fine dining but the fixed menu locals' lunch is good value at £25 for 3 courses. Booking advised.

BYLAND ABBEY TEAROOM, YO61 4BD (01347 868204) Tea room and upmarket B&B beside the abbey ruins.

THE STAPYLTON ARMS, Wass YO61 4BE (01347 868280) Family-run gastropub with rooms.

Plenty of choice in Helmsley: **MANNION** (YO62 5AB, 01439 770044) is a high-end deli and bakery; **SCOTTS** (YO62 5BG, 01439 772465) for award-winning fish and chips; the **WALLED GARDEN CAFÉ** (YO62 5AH, 01439 771427) is in a splendid Victorian glasshouse; **HELMSLEY BREWERY** has a small taproom (YO62 5DX, 01439 771014); and **THE FEATHERS** is a big pub-hotel (YO62 5BH, 01439 770275).

HIGH PARADISE FARM, Boltby YO7 2HT (01845 537353) Rural B&B, tearoom and semi-wild camping, only accessible by bike and on foot.

BIKE SHOPS: Venture Cycles, Thirsk YO7 1LB (01845 868080). Sutton Bank Bikes, Sutton Bank National Park Centre YO7 2EH (01845 597759) Bike shop with full range of hire bikes including kids' bikes, trailers and e-bikes.

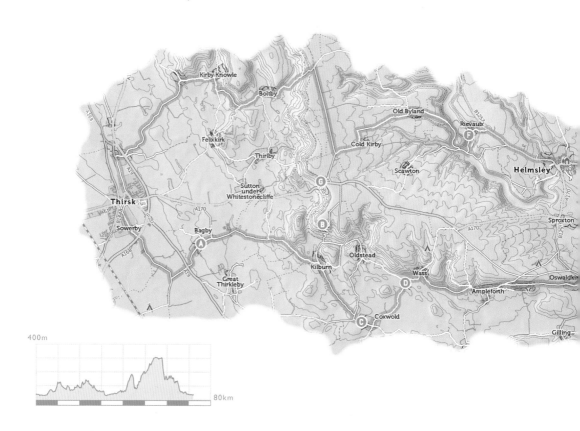

Walled Garden Café, Helmsley

Rievaulx

Shandy Hall

THE WAY OF THE WOLDS

From the ancient city of York to the highest village in Yorkshire's big sky country

———

The rolling hills – the wolds - of the East Riding of Yorkshire are the only chalk landscapes in Northern England. The geology of the North is so often characterised by millstone grit, limestones and volcanic lavas that it's an odd feeling suddenly to encounter downland, one of the signature landscapes of the South. But here it is in Yorkshire: mile upon mile of smooth, green whaleback hills, dry river valleys, pretty village greens and duck ponds. It makes for great cycling, as there are plenty of quiet lanes and byways. This ride can be paired with Ride No. 17 to make a tour of the length of the Wolds from York to Bridlington and back.

Starting at Monk Bar in York, the ride follows the most efficient way out of the city along Stockton Lane and takes in a short section of bridleway to stay off the busy main roads. The River Derwent is a natural barrier to travel in this part of the Vale of York; the route crosses the river at Howsham Ⓐ. In the grounds of Howsham Hall (a Jacobean pile said to be cursed as it was built with material from nearby Kirkham Priory) is an unusual Georgian Gothic watermill. It has recently been restored from dilapidation by the Renewable Energy Trust who run it as an education centre and have installed two Archimedes' screw turbines which supply hydroelectricity to the National Grid. The mill island is accessible on foot via a short track under the bridge and along the riverbank. The mill building itself is open to visitors on Sundays.

From Howsham the route strikes decisively woldward through Leavening and climbs the scarp slope of Leavening Brow Ⓑ. At the top, on the land surrounding Aldro Farm, is a concentration of prehistoric earthworks – Late Neolithic burial barrows and Bronze Age ditches and dykes thought to be part of the farming systems of the time. From this high point comes an astonishingly lovely descent down Water Dale, the only dry valley in the Wolds with a road running its full length. At the bottom is Thixendale with its one-room pub and even smaller village store. On summer Sundays, tea and cake are served in the village hall. But of course!

The Wolds get far fewer visitors than the Lakes, the Dales or the North York Moors, but nobody has done more to raise the profile of the Wolds than David Hockney. In the early 2000s, Hockney returned to Yorkshire from Los Angeles and made his home in Bridlington. For the next few years he drew, painted, photographed and filmed the lanes, fields, trees and hedgerows of the Wolds and brought a well-kept secret of the English countryside to a global audience of art fans. A website (Yocc.co.uk) shows the various

---

START & FINISH: York • DISTANCE: 57 miles / 91km • TOTAL ASCENT: 553m
TERRAIN: Mostly lanes and tarmac cycleway, one short off-road track. Moderate.

Wolds locations that Hockney painted. Fans will want to visit the location of his painting "Three Trees Near Thixendale": the trees are two miles east of the village in William Dale Ⓒ, on the road that leads north to the abandoned medieval village of Wharram Percy Ⓓ. It is well worth a detour if you have time and energy. But choices have to be made, and from Thixendale village the route turns south into Thixendale Wold.

The chalk landscape of the Wolds has a lot in common with its southern cousins but look closely and you'll soon find difference and distinctiveness. There's little or no flint-facing in the buildings, but much more limestone. The farming system is topsy-turvy with sheep and cattle grazing the valley floors while the uplands are ploughed for arable crops. Just like the downs, you need to get

up high to experience the Wolds at their wildest and most energising, from shimmering summer heatwaves to ferocious Siberian easterlies with everything in between.

Huggate is the highest village in the Wolds, so all roads from here go downhill. This the connecting point with Ride No. 17 to the coast at Bridlington (just follow the Way of the Roses / NCR 164 for 15 miles to Driffield). The descent from Huggate to Pocklington is another cracking cycling road along a dry river valley, passing the picture-postcard village of Millington. In the early summer months of May, June and July look out for scarlet drifts of wild poppies. Pocklington is a small, handsome market town, and marks the transition out of the Wolds and back into the flatlands of the Vale of York.

For the return to York the main objective is to dodge the main roads. The route picks a way through farmland, taking in a short section of rough stuff past the remains of the North Selby coal mine Ⓔ. Developed in the 1980s and 90s, the Selby coalfield was the last hurrah of the British coal industry with five mines sunk over an area of 20 square miles that were linked together underground. The shaft at Selby North was sunk to a depth of 1,034m, one of the deepest in Britain. There are now plans to turn the colliery site into a caravan park and campsite.

The final miles back to York are largely traffic-free along York's Solar System cycleway (formerly a section of the East Coast Main Line), past the racecourse on the Knavesmire and into the city centre along the River Ouse.

PUBS & PIT STOPS

JOLLY FARMERS INN, Leavening YO17 9SA (01653 658276) Village pub serving local ales and good food at weekend lunchtimes.

In Thixendale the tiny **CROSS KEYS** pub (YO17 9TG, 01377 288272) also does B&B. On Sundays there are teas at the village hall. Across the road, third-generation postmistress Maude Smith has been running the tiny village store for over 40 years.

WOLDS INN, Huggate YO42 1YH (01377 288217) No-nonsense country boozer with B&B rooms.

THE GAIT INN, Millington YO42 1TX (01759 302045) Rustic inn serving real ales and traditional pub fare.

RAMBLERS' REST, Millington YO42 1TX (01759 305292) Much-loved tea room and B&B in a picture-postcard village.

SWIRLZ, Pocklington YO42 2AS (07881 525054) Top-notch Italian-style gelato.

MARKET TAP, Pocklington YO42 2AS (01759 307783) Modern alehouse, food served.

RAILWAY STREET FISHERIES, Pocklington YO42 2QR (01759 302231) Traditional eat-in chippy.

York has a wealth of brilliant and historic pubs, among them the old school **GOLDEN BALL** (YO1 6DU, 01904 849040) and **BLUE BELL** (YO1 9TF, 01904 654904), the stylish alehouse **THE MALTINGS** (YO1 6HU, 01904 655387), the bizarre medieval **HOUSE OF THE TREMBLING MADNESS** (YO1 8AS, 01904 289848) and the grand **YORK TAP** in the railway station (YO24 1AB, 01904 659009).

BIKE SHOP: Cycle Heaven, York YO24 1AY (01904 622701) Bike hire available at the railway station branch. A bigger branch in the city centre.

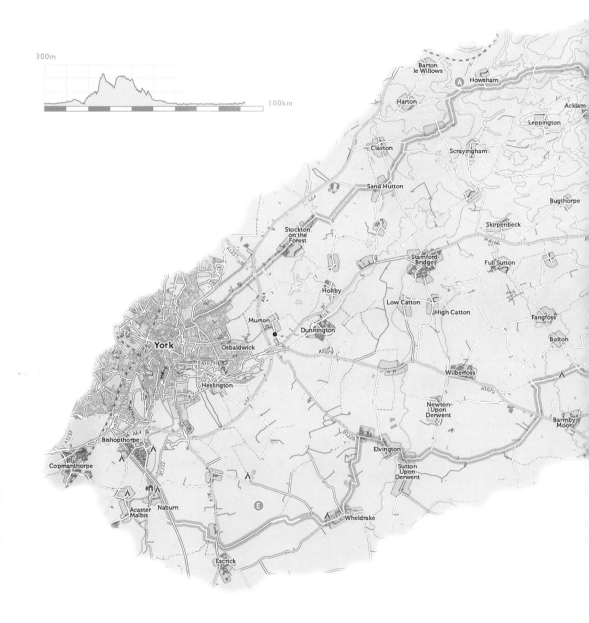

300m

100km

Barton le Willows
Howsham (A)
Harton
Acklam
Leppington
Claxton
Scrayingham
Sand Hutton
Bugthorpe
Skirpenbeck
Stockton on the Forest
Stamford Bridge
Full Sutton
Holtby
Low Catton
High Catton
Fangfoss
Murton
Dunnington
Bolton
York
Osbaldwick
Wilberfoss
A1079
Heslington
Newton Upon Derwent
Barmby Moor
Bishopthorpe
Elvington
Copmanthorpe
Sutton Upon Derwent
Acaster Malbis
Naburn
(E)
Wheldrake
Escrick

Wharram Percy

Monk Bar

HOCKNEY'S HINTERLAND

A tour of the big fields and old ways of the Yorkshire Wolds
taking in cliff tops and seafront

——

After returning from Los Angeles to his native Yorkshire in the early 2000s, David Hockney lived in Bridlington and embarked on an intensive period painting the lanes and byways he first got to know as a teenager growing up in Bradford. "I worked on a farm," he recalled. "I cycled around here for two summers. I used to cycle up to Scarborough, Whitby, a long way, actually. You get to know it, and you know it's hilly if you're cycling. I was always attracted to it. I always thought it had a space. One of the thrills of landscape is that it's a spatial experience." Two years of work resulted in *A Bigger Picture*, a blockbuster show at the Royal Academy. Ride No. 23 passes by Salt's Mill, in Saltaire, which boasts a huge collection of original Hockneys.

The present ride, together with Ride No. 16, forms a tour of the Wolds from York to Bridlington and back. But it works as a stand-alone route of 54 miles, though there are opportunities for short cuts.

The route starts and ends in Driffield, an unfussy market town that makes a good base for exploring both the Wolds and the flatlands of Yorkshire's east coast which, thanks to erosion and rising sea levels, has the fastest-disappearing coastline in Europe. Things begin in fine style, with a ride north out of Driffield on a lane up one of the dry river valleys that are a hallmark of the Wolds. Up on the ridge are the sites of two abandoned villages. Both date back over a thousand years and show the influence of Viking settlers. Little remains above ground, but the little church at Cowlam Ⓐ (hard by the farmyard) has an elaborately carved Romanesque font dating to around 1135 (there's another in nearby Langtoft), while the crumbling, red-brick Victorian church at Cottam is an eerie spot, especially when the crows are flapping about the place Ⓑ.

Across the B1249 is Woldgate, one of Yorkshire's great lost lanes. Once a Roman road from York to Bridlington, it was probably in use well before the Romans. This first section to Kilham is a fast downhill. The next village is Rudston, which means 'cross stone', and in the churchyard is the tallest standing stone in Britain Ⓒ. There's no clearer example of how Christianity adopted much older sacred sites and incorporated them into the new religion. The stone is almost eight metres tall (with a few more metres underground). It is oriented so that the broad side faces the sunrise at winter solstice and has been here for at least four thousand years. Early excavations found large numbers of buried skulls. Archaeologists believe it's the centrepiece of a larger sacred landscape of cursus and henge monuments that share many traits with those around Stonehenge.

START & FINISH: Driffield • DISTANCE: 54 miles / 85km • TOTAL ASCENT: 530m
TERRAIN: All lanes and a few urban roads in Bridlington. Moderate.

Rudston church

From Rudston it's ten miles on rolling farm lanes to the cliffs where the chalk mass of the Wolds comes to an abrupt end in the North Sea. Higher than the White Cliffs of Dover, Bempton Cliffs host a population of seabirds that from April to October can number half a million – the largest colony in England. Chief among them are gannets, guillemots, kittiwakes, shags and puffins. The grassland and scrub along the cliff tops are home to corn buntings, skylarks, linnets, reed buntings, rock and meadow pipits, willow warblers, chiffchaffs, sedge warblers and goldcrests. It is an RSPB nature reserve, and a small visitor centre gives the latest information on what's just flown in Ⓓ.

The cliffs continue all the way to the little cove at North Landing and the lighthouses at Flamborough Head. Both are worth a detour, not least to see the old lighthouse, built from blocks of chalk in 1674 and one of the oldest surviving lighthouses in England Ⓔ. The route follows NCR 1 to Sewerby Hall, a Georgian country house with dazzling formal gardens (£). The estate is home to a clifftop cricket ground from where a powerful batsman could probably loft the ball into the sea.

From here a car-free road leads onto the promenade at Bridlington. The town is the slightly dishevelled coastal cousin of elegant Scarborough and gothic Whitby that proudly proclaims itself as the lobster capital of Europe. More than 300 tonnes were landed here in 2019, mostly destined for France, Spain and Italy. If Brid, as locals call it, feels as though it suffers from an identity crisis, that's because it's the amalgamation of two settlements: the harbour and, nearly a mile inland, the Georgian Old Town built around the medieval priory.

From the priory, the Way of the Roses leads out of town, along the bypass, and onto Woldgate. After the traffic of Brid it's an unexpected oasis and a gloriously lost lane. It's amazing to think that this was once the main road to York. It's no surprise that David Hockney came back again and again to paint it in its changing seasons. When I rode along here I saw greenfinches and had a brief staring match with a hare.

From a high point on Woldgate at Rudston Beacon, it's downhill all the way back to Driffield. Hockney pilgrims with decent-sized tyres will want to make a short detour by continuing along Woldgate and taking the next turning onto Green Lane and Sandy Lane, where he painted his 'tunnel' series Ⓕ. If architecture is more your thing, then stick to the road route and stop in at Burton Agnes Hall (£), an Elizabethan mansion designed by Robert Smythson, whose other works include Longleat. Next door is the much older Burton Agnes Manor House, built in the 1170s. Ⓖ (EH, free). From here it's all easy riding through farmland and the villages of Harpham, Wansford and Skerne. On the way into Driffield the route passes Bell Mills, a huge red-brick flour mill that produces almost 3% of the country's flour, grinding 3,000 tonnes of wheat a week.

PUBS & PIT STOPS

THE OLD STAR, Kilham YO25 4RG (01262 420619) Traditional country pub, food served all day Thurs-Sun.

ANVIL ARMS, Wold Newton YO25 3YL (01262 470279) Off-route, a popular village pub with hearty, pie-oriented food.

CAFÉ KIOSK, RSPB Bempton Cliffs YO15 1JF (01262 422212) Hot drinks and snacks.

SHIP INN, Sewerby YO15 1EW (01262 672374) Bike-friendly pub with modern pub grub.

Plenty of choice in Bridlington: **NORTH BEACH FISH AND CHIPS** on Marine Drive (YO15 2NB), **SUPATTRA** (YO15 2AR, 01262 678565) for superior Thai food; the **GEORGIAN ROOMS** (YO16 4QA, 01262 608600) is a tea room in pretty Old Town; the beautifully preserved **STATION BUFFET** railway refreshment room for teas and coffees (YO15 3EP, 01262 673709).

COURTYARD CAFÉ, Burton Agnes Hall YO25 4NE (01262 490324) Snacks, light meals and ice cream with outside seating.

ST. QUINTIN ARMS, Harpham YO25 4QY (01262 490329) Whitewashed coaching inn with good, meaty food. Rooms.

THE BUTCHER'S DOG, Driffield YO25 6PS (01377 252229) Micropub with good ales and pork pies.

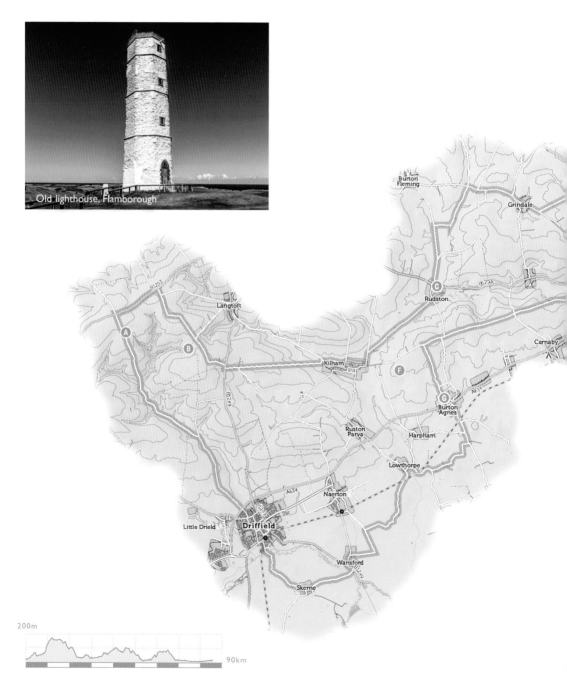

Old lighthouse, Flamborough

Burton
Fleming

Grindale

Langtoft

Rudston

Carnaby

Ⓐ

Ⓑ

Kilham

Ⓕ

Ⓖ

Burton
Agnes

Ruston
Parva

Harpham

Lowthorpe

Naerton

Little Drield

Driffield

Wansford

Skerne

200m

90km

Cottam church

Bempton cliffs

YORKSHIRE
DALES

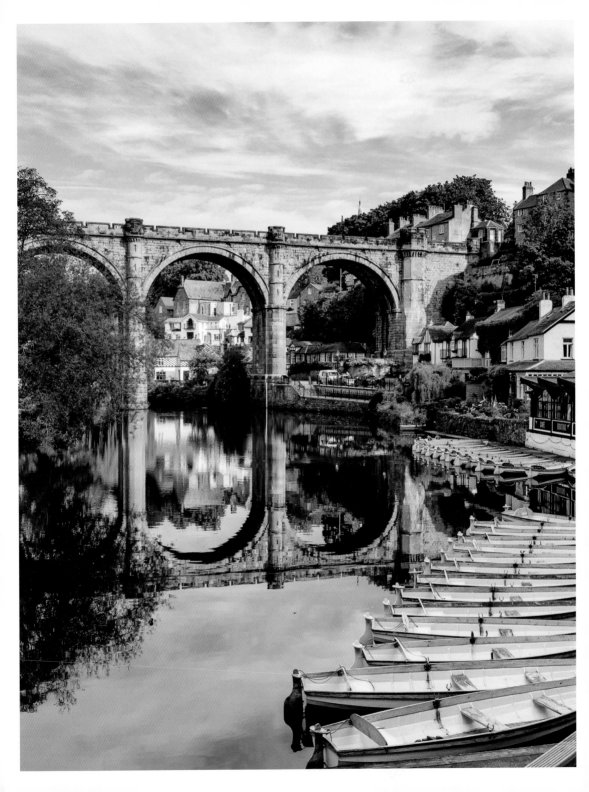

SONG OF STONE

From elegant Harrogate to the edge of the Yorkshire Dales,
with magnificent architecture around every corner

———

Harrogate is one of the few British spa towns that still has a spa. People have come here to 'take the waters' since the early 17th century. When they opened in 1897, the town's Turkish baths were considered spectacular, with Islamic-influenced design, colourful glazed tiles, Italian mosaic floors and the finest brass and mahogany fittings. Thanks to a meticulous restoration, the baths are every bit as plush a century later. Whether you're an aficionado of steam and the ice-cold plunge, or simply curious about exactly what happens at a Turkish bath, this is the place to go. It's also a perfect way to soothe tired muscles after a day out on the bike.

At the turn of the 20th century Harrogate was a playground of the European elite. This is a little hard to imagine as you head out of town along the railway line, through the Asda car park and in and out of various industrial estates. But such is the way of the National Cycle Network. Things soon get better as you turn onto the Beryl Burton Cycleway Ⓐ. This part of the larger Nidderdale Greenway connects Harrogate with neighbouring Knaresborough and is named for Yorkshire's most successful cyclist. Burton won more than 90 domestic championships and seven world titles, and dominated the sport like no rider before or since. Her British record for the 12-hour time trial surpassed the men's record.

Knaresborough might just be the most spectacular town in Yorkshire. It's set in a steep wooded gorge with a railway viaduct leaping across the River Nidd. Amazingly, the viaduct collapsed shortly before completion and had to be completely rebuilt. Its elaborate castellated style divides opinion among architectural critics. Pevsner loathed it, Priestley loved it. You decide who was right.

As good as the view is from the riverside, it's even better from the castle – if you're up to climbing the steps just behind the Riverside Café. From here it's north through the town centre out into the wheat fields. Quiet lanes lead to Ripon, whose whopping cathedral took three hundred years to build. Like the viaduct at Knaresborough it suffered a collapse, following an earthquake in 1450. Christianity goes back a long way here, this being the fourth church built on the site. The Saxon crypt, built in 672AD and said to be modelled on the tomb of Jesus Christ, predates the creation of England by 255 years. Now that's old. Imposing, but in a different way, are Ripon's courthouse, prison and workhouse. All three are run as museums (£) and even if you don't stop they're worth a look from the outside.

A few miles on is Studley Royal Park which encompasses a Georgian landscaped park and

START & FINISH: Harrogate • DISTANCE: 42 miles / 67km • TOTAL ASCENT: 663m
TERRAIN: Lanes and tarmac cycleway. Moderate.

Nidderdale Greenway

water gardens, a large Elizabethan country house and the ruined remains of Fountains Abbey ⑧. Once the largest and wealthiest monastery in England, the ruins are now owned by the National Trust. When visiting by bike it's easiest to use the west entrance, half a mile beyond the main visitor centre. If you're not going in, there's a good view of the abbey from the left side of the lane on the little rise after crossing the River Skell.

Six miles on is another architectural master-piece, no less amazing for the fact that it has no architect but the wind and the rain, the rivers and tides of thousands of years. Brimham Rocks is an outcrop of hard millstone grit that survived the Ice Age and the glacier that carved out the Nidd Valley from other, softer rocks. Standing above the glacier, howling icy gales carved the rock

into weird and wonderful shapes and left massive boulders balancing in improbable positions. Entrance is free if you've come by bike ©.

Very much man-made, and clearly visible on the horizon to the south, are the giant spherical radomes of Menwith Hill. A top-secret facility run by the United States with British support, it is said to be the largest electronic surveillance station in the world and part of a global spy network with the power to eavesdrop on every phone call and email anywhere on the planet. It's also alleged that US military drone attacks are coordinated from the base.

The final leg of the ride back to Harrogate follows the path of the glacier down the Nidd Valley, passing through the grounds of Ripley Castle, home of the Ingilby family since 1309 ⑩. In the mid-19th century the estate village was remodelled in an ornate Gothic Revival style, inspired by villages in the Alsace. The stone lettering above the town hall reads "Hotel de Ville".

From Ripley it's the 4-mile, traffic-free Nidderdale Greenway all the way back to Harrogate. The cycleway uses the trackbed of an old railway. It passes through the Nidd Gorge, a slice of neglected and overlooked 'edgeland' that's the setting for local author Rob Cowen's 2015 book *Common Ground*, which has become a touchstone in new nature writing. The gorge has long been under threat from a planned new relief road, but local campaigners recently triumphed and the council dropped the proposal.

It's the same unglamorous route back into Harrogate town centre but it won't matter as by now your mind will have turned to a well-earned steam and sauna session at the Turkish baths.

PUBS & PIT STOPS

RIVERSIDE CAFÉ, Knaresborough (HG5 8DE, 01423 546759) Riverside café popular with local cyclists.

Good options in Ripon: **REALITEA** (HG4 1DP, 01765 609887) is a unique café-bistro serving Indian tapas and homemade cakes; **CHIMES CAFÉ** (HG4 1PA, 01765 606167) is close by the cathedral, and the **ROYAL OAK** (HG4 1PB, 01765 602284) is a stylish pub with rooms serving Timothy Taylor ales and above-average food.

BOAR'S HEAD, Ripley HG3 3AY (01423 771888) Handsome, ivy-clad coaching inn. Rooms.

TURKISH BATHS, Harrogate HG1 2WH (01423 556746) Perfect post-ride relaxation.

BETTYS CAFÉ TEA ROOMS, Harrogate HG1 2QU (01423 814070) A Yorkshire institution since 1919. Grand architecture and traditional afternoon tea.

There are some good pubs and bars in Harrogate including **MAJOR TOM'S SOCIAL** (HG1 2RB, 01423 566984) which serves bistro-type food, the **LITTLE ALE HOUSE** (HG1 1DH, 07792 175380) for craft ales and pork pies; and the **HARROGATE TAP** (HG1 1TE, 01423 501644) in the railway station.

BIKE SHOPS: Chevin Cycles, Harrogate HG1 2BF (01423 568222) Big bike shop, e-bike hire available. Moonglu, Ripon HG4 2AN (01765 601106). Vern Overton Cycling, Darley HG3 2QN (07595 460465) Bike and e-bike hire in nearby Nidderdale.

300m

70km

Ripley castle

Brimham Rocks

Studley Royal

Fountains Abbey

THREE PEAKS

Yorkshire's famous trio of flat-topped hills are the backdrop
to this ride around the headwaters of the River Ribble

———

The Three Peaks of Ingleborough, Whernside and Pen-y-ghent are the best-known hills in the Yorkshire Dales. It's a popular walking challenge to do all three in a day, and once a year they host Britain's biggest and toughest cyclo-cross race. The race sees hundreds of men and women ride, push, carry, slip and slide their way around the gruelling course, which includes all three summits. This ride takes the iconic hills as its backdrop but keeps to the surfaced lanes, though there are still a few testing hills to contend with.

Settle is my favourite town in the Yorkshire Dales. There's a railway station, a Victorian music hall, a handsome market square (Tuesday is market day), a tiny town museum and a good bike shop. Unlike some Dales villages that are overrun by tourists, you sense that Settle exists primarily for its own townsfolk, though visitors are quite welcome to join in, too. The town stands beside the young River Ribble and the ride begins by heading north up the valley.

Turning west towards Austwick is a lane that for a few short miles delivers everything that is wonderful about cycling in the Yorkshire Dales: narrow lanes, neat stone walls and field barns, and cattle and sheep grazing a jigsaw of small fields beneath limestone crags. After the briefest encounter with the A65 the back lanes continue

through Clapham, home of the Farrer family whose Ingleborough Estate owns much of the land around here. Born in 1880, Reginald Farrer was a botanist and globetrotting plant collector. He is recognised as a forefather of the 'naturalistic' style of gardening that holds sway today. In one experiment he used a shotgun to launch seeds collected from the Himalayas into a cliff face in the Dales. If you see a sprawling rhododendron or a clump of bamboo growing by the roadside, or get a scented whiff from the delicate pink-white flowers of *Viburnum farreri*, it may well be a descendant of a specimen brought back from one of his daredevil journeys. He died aged 40 while on a plant-hunting expedition in Burma, most probably having contracted diphtheria.

Beyond Clapham are the pastured lower slopes of Ingleborough, the first of the Three Peaks, though its summit remains tantalisingly out of view. Ingleton is a centre for caving and outdoor adventure activities as the whole area is a geological Swiss cheese, run through with caves, potholes, underground rivers and waterfalls. Beyond Ingleton lies Kingsdale. There's no royal connection: the name is a combination of Old Norse *kyen* and Old English *dael* and means the 'valley where the cows are kept'. The valley rises to the highest point of the ride at the pass between

---

START & FINISH: Settle • DISTANCE: 47 miles / 75km • TOTAL ASCENT: 1073m
TERRAIN: All lanes. Moderate/Challenging.

Kingsdale

Dent

Whernside and Crag Hill. This is the border between North Yorkshire and Cumbria and looks out onto a geological divide, being the transition from the limestone block of the Yorkshire Dales to the much older sandstones of the Howgill Fells.

It's all downhill to Dent which is like rolling into a cobblestoned time warp, if you can ignore the passing traffic. Dent's most famous son is Adam Sedgwick, one of the founders of modern geology. At Cambridge he taught the young Charles Darwin, though, as a devout Christian and priest, he disputed Darwin's theory of evolution. A slab of pink Shap granite in the centre of the village is engraved with his name Ⓐ.

It's now east up Dentdale, following the River Dee, which has some good swimming spots, though they can dry up in the summer months. Further up the valley the Settle-Carlisle railway

emerges from a tunnel to leap the gorge on the Dent Viaduct. At the very top of the climb is the bare hollow of Newby Head Moss and the junction with the B6255. To the north it goes to Hawes (a connection with Ride No. 21) but our route turns south to Ribblehead.

The Ribble may be the great river of Lancashire but it starts its journey here in Yorkshire and the rest of the ride follows its course back to Settle. Altogether overshadowing the source of the river is the Ribblehead Viaduct, probably the most impressive man-made object in the Yorkshire Dales Ⓑ. The Settle-Carlisle line was the last railway to have been built by gangs of navvies armed with little more than picks and shovels. A quarter of a mile long, the 24 arches carry the railway across a broad valley with the implausibly uber-Yorkshire name of Batty Moss. The viaduct took five years to build with a workforce of around two thousand men. It cost the lives of over a hundred of them – both from accidents and from diseases like smallpox and typhoid which were endemic in the shanty towns that sprang up around the construction site.

With Ingleborough to the right and Pen-y-ghent to the left, the run down Ribblesdale to Settle is a classic. However, one signature Dales landscape that is not really visible from the road is its limestone pavements. Also known as karst, they are an eerie moonscape with rare and delicate flora that cling on in the poor, alkaline soil. To see one up close, head off-road to the Ingleborough Nature Reserve at Sulber. It's a mile's walk or ride along the Pennine Bridleway – a right turn just past the hamlet of Selside Ⓒ.

From Helwith Bridge the route takes the quiet way back. On a hot summer's day, the plunge pools and sunny limestone slabs around Stainforth Force waterfalls are a popular wild swimming spot with a large, deep pool about 150m downstream. Just turn left in Little Stainforth, where there's also riverside camping Ⓓ.

PUBS & PIT STOPS

READING ROOM, Clapham LA2 8EQ (015242 51144) Café, bar and bunk barn.

BERNIE'S, Ingleton LA6 3EB (0330 113 9848) Outdoorsy café serving food from breakfast to teatime.

STONE CLOSE TEA ROOM, Dent LA10 5QL (01539 625231) Cosy tea room and good value B&B.

THE SUN INN, Dent LA10 5QL (01539 625208) Quintessential Dales village pub. Rooms.

THE SPORTSMAN'S INN, Cowgill LA10 5RG (01539 625282) Whitewashed 17th-century inn with flagstone floors, good food. Ewegales Farm campsite nearby.

HELWITH BRIDGE INN, Helwith Bridge BD24 0EH (01729 860220) Real ale pub by the river with basic camping.

KNIGHTS TABLE, Little Stainforth BD24 0DP (01729 822200) Surprisingly good café-bar in this sprawling riverside camping and caravan site.

WOODEND FARM CAMPING, Austwick LA2 8DH (015242 51296) Small riverside site with good facilities.

Plenty of choice in Settle: **SYDNEY'S** tapas bar (BD24 9EF, 01729 822000) makes a change from the usual; **TALBOT ARMS** (BD24 9EX, 01729 823924) is a family-run free house, while the **GOLDEN LION** (BD24 9DU, 01729 822203) is an upmarket coaching inn with rooms; **YE OLDE NAKED MAN CAFÉ** (BD24 9ED, 01729 823230) is a no-frills favourite.

BIKE SHOP: 3 Peaks Cycles, Settle BD24 9EJ (01729 824232) Bike shop and café. Full range of hire bikes.

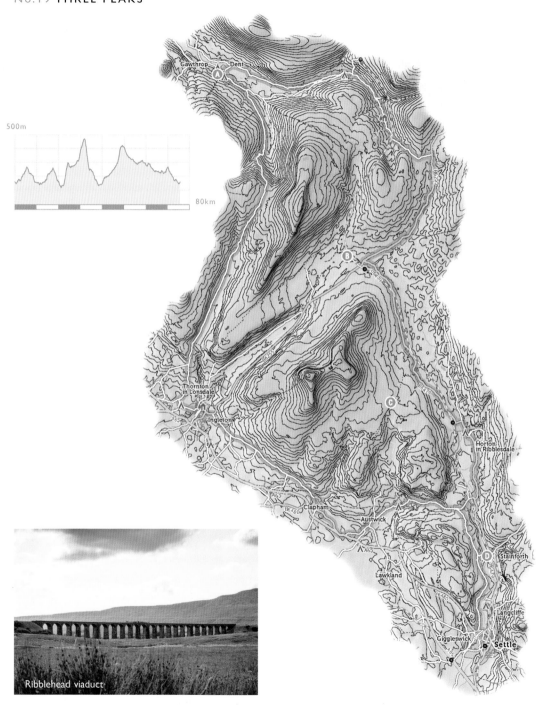

500m

80km

Gawthrop
Dent
A

B

C

Thornton
in Lonsdale

Ingleton

Horton
in Ribblesdale

Clapham

Austwick

D Stainforth

Lawkland

Langcliffe

Giggleswick

Settle

Ribblehead viaduct

Dent Head viaduct

River Dent

UP HILL DOWN DALE

Big views and tough climbs among the magnificent
limestone rock formations of the Yorkshire Dales

————

The Rough-Stuff Fellowship is the oldest off-road cycling club in the world. It was founded in 1957, long before Northern Californians in check shirts took their clunkers on the dirt tracks of Marin County and invented mountain biking. RSF members sought out the green lanes, drove roads and mountain tracks of the British Isles and ventured into still wilder places like the Alps, Norway and Iceland, even taking bikes to the foot of Mount Everest. This ride takes in a short section of Mastiles Lane, an all-time classic rough stuff route that, before it was discovered by men and women riding steel bikes with canvas saddlebags, woollen socks and brass Primus stoves, was once a Roman road and an important medieval trade route across the Dales.

Starting from Settle, the route heads straight uphill, as is often the way in the Dales. Fortunately, there's a good excuse to take a break from the effort in the form of Scaleber Force, a waterfall set in dense woodland, just a short walk from the road Ⓐ. Further up the hill are big views south across Ribblesdale into Lancashire. The dark, glowering form of Pendle Hill is quite visible in the distance. There are more good views on the long descent to Airton beside the young River Aire. The river rises in the Dales and flows south into the industrial West Riding and through the

centre of Leeds before joining the Ouse on its slow, meandering way to the North Sea. Here in the Dales it's a fast-flowing stream, rushing and tumbling through the limestone.

Dramatic limestone is the defining feature of the next section, through Malham and up to Mastiles Lane, passing some of the most remarkable geology of the Dales. It's visible in all directions, but the two highlights are Janet's Foss and Gordale Scar. Janet's Foss is a small but enchanting waterfall and swimmable plunge pool about a mile beyond Malham Ⓑ (the footpath is clearly signed). On the far side of the stone bridge is Gordale Scar. It's a 500-yard walk from the road through a small campsite, clearly signed Ⓒ. A huge wall of limestone, like the crumbling ruins of a giant's fortress, it's awe-inspiring, especially when you remember that it is all made from the crushed and compacted remains of microscopic sea creatures that lived in shallow seas hundreds of millions of years ago. Geologists are unclear how Gordale Scar came into being. Some believe it to be a collapsed cave system that was formed during an earlier ice age.

The road continues uphill, getting ever steeper until the landscape opens up into the broad moorland tops. Here you'll feel quite alone as you venture onto the unsurfaced track and join Mastiles

---

START & FINISH: Settle • DISTANCE: 39 miles / 63km • TOTAL ASCENT: 968m
TERRAIN: Mostly lanes and one short section of rough stuff. Moderate/Challenging.

Littondale

River Wharfe

Mastiles Lane

Lane ⓓ. The full length of the road runs from just east of Malham Tarn for five miles eastwards to the village of Kilnsey. It passes through a Roman marching camp and is flanked by stone walls for much of the way. In medieval times this was the route taken by the monks of Fountains Abbey (see Ride No. 18) to reach their valuable sheep grazing lands in the Dales and beyond. If you want to follow the track east to Kilnsey and are prepared for some more rough stuff, that is possible and will trim a few miles from the route.

Easier and equally scenic is the tarmac lane to the south-west towards Threshfield and on into Grassington. Here, in the valley of the River Wharfe, another of Yorkshire's great rivers, you'll swap the wild solitude of Mastiles Lane for the hordes of day trippers that tend to overpower this pretty Dales village, especially in summer. Even so, the Grassington Folk Museum is worth a visit (free entry) and there are some good swim spots on the river. The most popular of these is Linton Falls, a little way downstream of the road bridge ⓔ. The easiest access by bike is via the path at the bottom of the car park at the National Park Centre. There is a footpath along the river bank.

From Grassington, the route continues upstream, passing beneath the dramatic overhang of Kilnsey Crag. The route then forks left into Littondale (fork right to connect with Ride No. 21). Littondale is an archetypal glacial U-shaped valley and it's a gem of a road to ride. Just off-route is Arncliffe, so obviously a Dales village that it was used as the filming location for the first seasons of Emmerdale Farm in the early 1970s ⓕ. Production was soon moved to Esholt to be closer to the Yorkshire TV studios in Leeds; the show is now filmed in a purpose-built set on the Harewood Estate.

At the head of the valley the road makes a sharp turn before climbing through stone-walled fields onto the open moor. At the top there's a good view of Pen-y-ghent, the smallest but most mountain-like of the Yorkshire Three Peaks. All three are isolated remnants of an entire layer of millstone grit that once lay on top of the older Carboniferous limestone.

If Mastiles Lane gave you a taste for the rough stuff, there are a couple of decent rough stuff options off to the right. (The first, Long Lane via Churn Milk Hole, is the rougher of the two while the second, Moor Head Lane from just past Sannat Hall Farm, is a good gravel track.) Either one would be a more adventurous alternative to the road back down into Ribblesdale Ⓖ. Once back in the valley, I prefer the quieter back lane for the last miles into Settle, with the bonus of one last five-star swim spot at Stainforth Force Ⓗ.

PUBS & PIT STOPS

TOWN END FARM SHOP, Airton BD23 4BE (01729 830902) Award-winning farm shop and tea room.

LISTER ARMS, Malham BD23 4DB (01729 830444) Large country inn serving hearty fare. Well-appointed rooms.

GORDALE SCAR CAMPING, BD23 4DL (01729 830333) Basic riverside campsite in a stunning location near the geological wonder.

FOUNTAINE INN, Linton BD23 5HJ (01756 752210) Smart country pub with comfortable rooms.

TENNANTS ARMS, Kilnsey BD23 5PS (01756 753946) Swanky Dales dining pub with elegant rooms.

THE FALCON INN, Arncliffe BD23 5QE (01756 770205) The original Woolpack in Emmerdale Farm. Total time warp: beer straight from the cask, pie and peas lunch. B&B available.

THE QUEENS ARMS, Litton BD23 5QJ (01756 770096) Foodie pub, own-brewed beer, good value rooms.

THE KNIGHTS TABLE, Little Stainforth BD24 0DP (01729 822200) Surprisingly good café-bar in this sprawling riverside camping and caravan site.

Plenty of choice in Settle: **SYDNEY'S** tapas bar (BD24 9EF, 01729 822000) makes a change from the usual; the **TALBOT ARMS** (BD24 9EX, 01729 823924) is a family-run free house, while the **GOLDEN LION** (BD24 9DU, 01729 822203) is an upmarket coaching inn with rooms; **YE OLDE NAKED MAN CAFÉ** (BD24 9ED, 01729 823230) is a no-frills favourite.

BIKE SHOP: 3 Peaks Cycles, Settle BD24 9EJ (01729 824232) Bike shop and café. Full range of hire bikes.

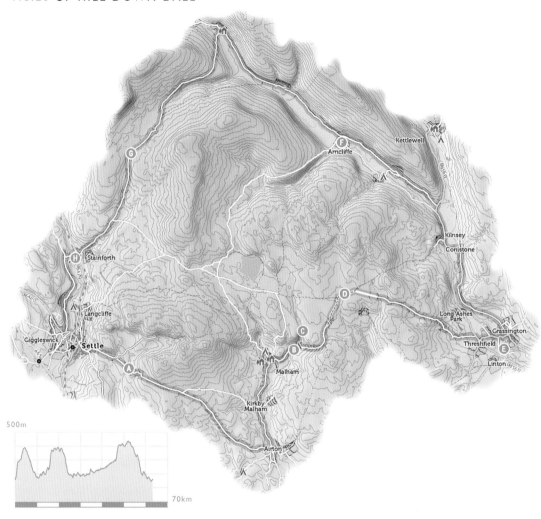

500m

70km

The Falcon Inn, Arncliffe

Goredale Scar

A GRAND DAY OUT

A climber's feast starting in Wensleydale, heart of the Dales,
taking in two of its classic roads

———

It's accepted wisdom among experienced cyclists that when riding over a big hill it's preferable to ride up the steeper slope and then coast down the shallower side. It's part psychology and part physics. A short, sharp and steep climb is over sooner than an interminably long uphill drag, and you get the full benefit of the hard work in a long easy descent and don't have to waste energy braking as you might on a very steep descent. And if you have to walk up, it's a short walk.

That's the theory anyway and, if it sounds counter-intuitive, this ride gives you the perfect opportunity to put it to the test. It includes Fleet Moss and Park Rash, two of the most celebrated climbs in the Yorkshire Dales, taking both of them the 'hard way' followed by glorious, long descents through the sumptuous Dales landscapes.

Starting at Hawes, the capital of Upper Wensleydale, the route heads straight uphill past the front door of the Wensleydale Creamery where the famous Yorkshire cheese is produced (tours are available, £). Poor sales of Wensleydale cheeses in the early 1990s meant the creamery was about to close. Then the Wallace and Gromit clay animations came along. Wallace proclaims Wensleydale to be his favourite cheese and – amazingly – the free publicity reversed the company's fortunes.

This climb is Fleet Moss, Yorkshire's highest road and a landmark in British cycling Ⓐ. It's a long climb that gets steeper the further you go on, so take it easy and save some energy for the second half where the gradient gets close to 20%. Near the top of the steepest section, the road crosses a much older Roman road, now a bridleway known as the Cam High Road, which connects Bainbridge with Ribblehead. It's one of the classic rough stuff routes in the Dales.

It's difficult to work out where the top of Fleet Moss actually is but soon enough you'll be coasting down the other side, and then it's downhill all the way to Kettlewell, 11 miles away. The landscape is little changed from the late-17th century, when a combination of high prices for livestock, and cash-strapped aristocratic landowners led to a building boom as farmers bought their own parcels of land. They divided up the lower-lying pasture into rectangular plots bounded by stone walls and built neat, two-storey field barns to overwinter cattle and store hay. The uplands were for open grazing, though this was strictly regulated with each farmer having an allocation measured in 'gaits' (one gait was the land required to graze one sheep; a cow required four gaits and a horse eight gaits). Much of Langstrothdale is now owned by the National Trust, and the Landmark

START & FINISH: Hawes • DISTANCE: 48 miles / 77km • TOTAL ASCENT: 1185m
TERRAIN: All lanes. Challenging.

Fleet Moss

Park Rash

Trust has restored Cowside, a rare unaltered example of a late-17th century farmhouse, which is available as a holiday let Ⓑ.

Curiously named Hubberholme was described by novelist J.B. Priestley as the "smallest, pleasantest place in the world" and his ashes are buried in the churchyard. The church itself has one of only two medieval carved rood-screens and lofts in the North to have survived the Reformation, as well as some good carved wooden pews. Like many rivers in the Dales, the Wharfe often runs dry, but there are some excellent spots for a quick dip when the water's flowing. A good one is downstream of the footbridge at Starbotton Ⓒ.

Kettlewell is a village at the crossroads and a popular spot for walkers, cyclists and motorbikers to stop for refreshments. This may be a wise move as the route now turns north and begins the

climb over to Coverdale. It's steep immediately out of the village but there's much, much worse to come. When I caught my first sight of the hairpins of Park Rash, I thought there had been some mistake. No road could possibly go up there. But go up there it does, and it's a beast of a climb, with the first few ramps a brutal 25% Ⓓ.

Unlike Fleet Moss, the top of this climb has all the feeling of an Alpine pass, with big views in both directions, and a ten-mile descent down Coverdale to the village of Wensley which lends its name to Wensleydale. Standing guard over the valley is Castle Bolton (Ⓔ £). Built in the late-14th century, its box-like shape signals the transition of great houses from defensive structures to domestically oriented stately homes. It's part of the Bolton Estate whose lands include 5,000 acres of heather moor managed for grouse shooting. In a public-spirited policy, the estate tends to leave its shooting huts unlocked as shelters for wayfarers: Dent's Houses can be found off the road to Grinton, while Greets Shooting House and Stackhill House are off the roads above Askrigg. They are shown on the OS Explorer maps and are accessible via bridleways. The bothy code applies: bring your own firewood and leave the hut spick and span.

If a river swim is on the agenda, there are two excellent spots. Redmire Falls are a well-kept secret beside pastures, woodland and limestone cliffs; there are rope swings and some deep pools. Take the lane south of Redmire to Mill Farm then follow the footpath upstream for 500 yards Ⓕ. Aysgarth Falls are popular with the summer crowds and can be found downstream of the bridge south of Carperby Ⓖ.

The last few miles head west up Wensleydale and into the setting sun. Askrigg is a picture-perfect Dales village with its stone market cross and an old Cyclists' Touring Club sign on the pub. It still draws visitors as the setting of the wildly popular 1970s television series *All Creatures Great and Small*, based on the books by James Herriot (see also Ride No. 15).

PUBS & PIT STOPS

THE GEORGE INN, Hubberholme BD23 5JE (01756 760223) Pub in 17th-century farmhouse with award-winning pies. Rooms.

WEST WINDS TEAROOMS, Buckden BD23 5JA (01756 760883) Trad tearooms with reasonably priced rooms for overnight stays.

WHITE LION INN, Cray BD23 5JB (01756 760262) Just off-route, a real gem of a Dales pub with exceptional food and comfortable rooms.

KING'S HEAD, Kettlewell BD23 5RD (01756 761600) All three Kettlewell pubs are good but the Kings Head just edges it for food. Good value rooms.

ZARINA'S TEA ROOM, Kettlewell BD23 5QX (01756 761188) Quaint tea room. B&B available.

KETTLEWELL CAMPING, Kettlewell BD23 5RE (07930 379079) Small campsite in the village with good facilities and hot showers.

THWAITE ARMS, Horsehouse DL8 4TS (01969 640206) Really nice, out of the way Dales pub.

KINGS ARMS, Askrigg DL8 3HL (01969 650113) The Drovers in All Creatures Great and Small, bags of character.

GREEN DRAGON, Hardraw DL8 3LZ (01969 667392) Just off-route, atmospheric old inn with rooms & bunk house. Hardraw Force waterfall nearby, and a popular campsite.

BLACKBURN FARM CAMPING, Hawes DL8 3NX (01969 667524) Small farm campsite near Hawes, good views over Wensleydale.

BIKE SHOP: Stage 1 Cycles, Hawes DL8 3NT (01969 666873) Bike shop and café by the National Park Centre. Bike and e-bike hire available.

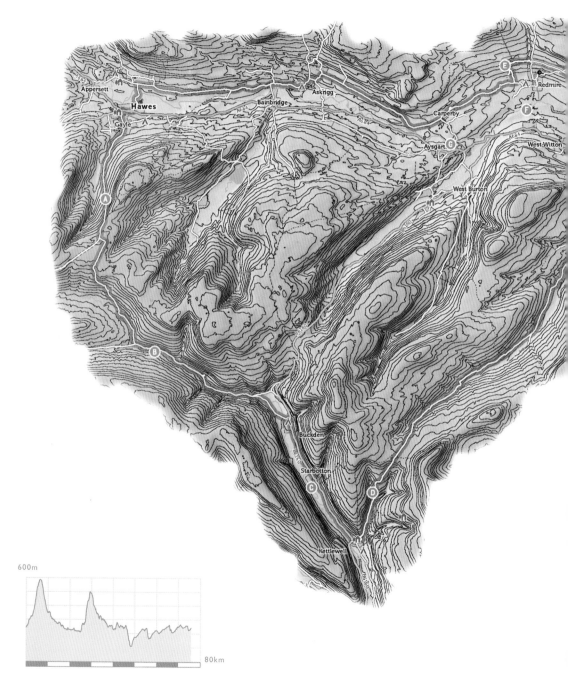

600m

80km

River Ure

Thwaite Arms, Horsehouse

Bolton Castle

SECRETS OF SWALEDALE

A ride up one of Yorkshire's best-loved dales and onto
the bleak moors around the highest pub in Britain

———

In just under 30 miles, this route takes in the three landscape types of the Yorkshire Dales: Upper Swaledale's lush patchwork of farmland; the wild, windswept moors around Tan Hill; and the old lead mining valley of Arkengarthdale. My route starts and finishes at Reeth, the largest settlement in Upper Swaledale, but it's quite possible to add a few extra miles (and hills) by riding over from Richmond via Marske in the east, or from Kirkby Stephen over the moors in the west.

The brilliant little volunteer-run museum of Swaledale in Reeth is a good place to start to get to grips with the geology, landscape and history of this corner of the Yorkshire Dales and will help make sense of what you will see along the way. Reeth grew as a town thanks to the lead mining boom of the late-18th and early 19th centuries. The population of Upper Swaledale and Arken-garthdale reached a peak of 7,500 in the 1820s; it's now less than a quarter of that.

Across the river from Reeth is the hamlet of Grinton and its outsized church which dates back almost a thousand years. It was once the only church in the valley and a medieval 'Corpse Way' runs all the way from the head of the valley at Keld, from where it was a two-day walk in which mourners bore their dead in a wicker coffin to save weight. West of Grinton the lane rises up the south side of the valley below the remains of an Iron Age hill fort known as Maiden Castle (it's a short walk uphill to get there) Ⓐ. The route up the valley mixes lanes with the better sections of the Swale Trail off-road cycle route. In places it can be loose under wheel: if you're on a road bike it's best to stick to the tarmac of the B6270.

Swaledale gave its name to the black-faced sheep that are a dominant breed in the Northern uplands, but it's dairy farming that explains the division of the valley into square fields with box-like field barns (or cow'uses – cow houses – as they're more authentically known). These were originally built to store hay made in the surrounding meadows and to house three or four cows during the winter. This traditional way of farming is no longer economically viable, and sheep ranching has largely taken over from hay meadows and dairying in the uplands.

It's possible to keep to the tarmac through Muker and Thwaite, both attractive Swaledale villages, but for a more adventurous alternative route to Keld, I prefer to cross the river to Ivelet and, when the lane ends, continue along the Corpse Way track up the narrow gorge, past the ruins of Crackpot Hall Ⓑ. The location is perfect and it must have been quite a place to live, until it was abandoned in the 1950s due to subsidence. Sheep

---

START & FINISH: Reeth • DISTANCE: 28 miles / 46km • TOTAL ASCENT: 767m
TERRAIN: On road and an optional 3-mile section of track that's rough in places. Moderate.

Crackpot Hall

and rabbits are the only residents now, but a 1930s book about the Dales tells of the Harker family and their "untamed children" who lived at Crackpot, wild and free as "spirits of the moors". No doubt they would have enjoyed the waterfall and wild swimming paradise of Kisdon Force, down in the gorge ⓒ. It's an unforgettably good rough stuff route, but wide tyres and a sense of adventure are recommended. In the hills above Crackpot Hall are old mine workings from the time when the Dales were a major centre of lead mining.

Kelda means spring or fountain in Old Norse and half a mile west of the hamlet of Keld, and easily accessible from the B6270, is Wain Wath Force, a ten-foot-wide waterfall and large plunge pool that's a popular wild swimming spot, though take care as the water can be icy-cold ⓓ. A little

further uphill on Stonesdale Lane is Currack Force, another big waterfall set in dense woods with a good plunge pool ⓔ. If you've come on the rough stuff route via Crackpot Hall you'll pass above the falls on the footbridge just before you rejoin the road.

From here the route leaves behind the pleasant pastures of Swaledale for a long, steady climb up Stonesdale to the Tan Hill Inn ⓕ. This is the highest pub in Britain and the pub has made much of this accolade, which puts it firmly on the tourist trail (as well as being on the Pennine Way footpath). But the snow ploughs parked up outside tell of harsh winters up here. Revellers celebrating New Year's Eve 2009 were snowed in at the pub for three days. Or at least that was their story. The pub owes its existence to coal mining, which went on here from the 13th century up to the 1920s, and the pub was once surrounded by miners' cottages, now demolished. Barren moorland stretches away to the A66 highway in the north. The road heading east – in fact an 18th-century turnpike built for the lead mines – is a lonely one.

Soon enough comes the descent into Arkengarthdale, where the tumbling waters of the Arkle Beck have worn through the limestone to reveal rich veins of lead ore. The Romans were mining lead here in the 2nd century, and it was worked continuously from early medieval times until as recently as the First World War. The evidence, in the form of gruffy ground, bell pits, hushes and associated waterworks, is everywhere, though mostly overgrown. Langthwaite was the centre of the local lead industry and is a lovely village with sturdy terraced cottages crowded around The Red Lion pub which, if it's open, is the perfect place for a drink before the last few miles back to Reeth.

PUBS & PIT STOPS

TWO DALES BAKERY, Reeth DL11 6SP (01748 905001) Slow-fermentation sourdoughs, other baked goods and café.

DALES BIKE CENTRE, Fremington DL11 6AW (01748 884908) Bike shop with café, bike hire and hostel-style accommodation.

BRIDGE INN, Grinton DL11 6HH (01748 884224) Old coaching inn, good food including game shot by the landlords. Basic rooms.

Good rustic accommodation around Keld: **RUKIN'S PARK LODGE** (DL11 6LJ, 01748 886274) is a campsite with ace views; **SWALEDALE YURTS** (DL11 6DZ, 01748 886159) has camping, bunk house and glamping including a hot tub; up the hill is remote **FRITH LODGE** B&B (DL11 6EB, 01748 886489), evening meals served.

TAN HILL INN, Long Causeway DL11 6ED (01833 533007) Highest pub in Britain, B&B and very basic camping.

CHARLES BATHURST INN, Langthwaite DL11 6EN (0333 700 0779) Big, popular inn with good locally sourced food and plush rooms.

THE RED LION, Langthwaite DL11 6RE (01748 884218) Tiny lead miners' pub serving Black Sheep ales, pies and basic bar food.

BIKE SHOP: Dales Bike Centre (see above).

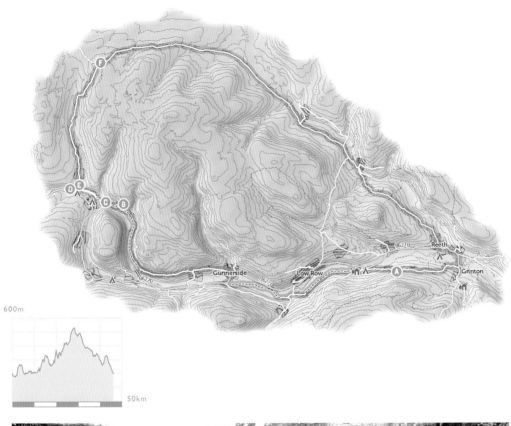

Keld

Tan Hill

WEST YORKSHIRE
& SOUTH
YORKSHIRE

A VERY YORKSHIRE JOURNEY

Grand civic architecture, windswept moors, industry, art and song:
it's all here in God's Own Country

———

"Don't talk to me about sophistication!" booms Harry Enfield's comedy Yorkshireman. "I've BEEN to Leeds!" This ride starts in the cloth town turned industrial city and commercial hub that few would deny has displaced medieval York to become the modern capital of God's Own Country, as Yorkshire patriots like to think of their homeland. It's a big and still-growing city with architecture to match, from Victorian civic and industrial masterpieces, to 1970s futurism and brutalism, to contemporary glass and steel.

The Aire Valley cuts a green swathe through the western half of the city and as well as the river, there's a road, a railway and a canal. On the way out of the city, the canal passes the back door of the excellent Leeds Industrial Museum Ⓐ (£). Housed in a handsome, late-Georgian woollen mill, it shows the complete manufacturing process. Two miles further along are the blackened ruins of Kirkstall Abbey (a little off-route on the far side of the River Aire, but entry is free so it's well worth a detour: access via an off-road track just by the war memorial on Bridge Road) Ⓑ.

Arriving in Saltaire along the canal is a thrill, with the towering mills rising like the walls of a canyon Ⓒ. Saltaire is the project of one man, Titus Salt, a Victorian mill owner from Bradford. As Salt's business grew, so did Bradford, from a rural backwater to the dirtiest town in the United Kingdom, according to one official report. The horrors of the factory system – low pay, long hours, child labour, overcrowding, incessant noise, choking smog, disease, the risk of fires in wooden buildings – were impossible to ignore. Like so many religious nonconformists of the time, Salt wanted to provide a better life for his workers. He bought a plot of land in the nearby Aire Valley where he would consolidate all his operations in new, fireproof buildings and provide his employees with good-quality homes, a hospital, a school, a library, parks, public baths and a grand Italianate church to worship in.

When it opened, Salt's Mill was the largest factory in Europe and its 3,000 workers could weave 18 miles of cloth a day. Salt was widely feted as the best face of Victorian capitalism. Yet there were critics. Rather than fix Bradford, he abandoned it. By owning a whole town he was able to control every aspect of the lives of his workers. Even so, when he died in 1876, it's said that 100,000 people lined the route of his funeral cortège. The core problem was the factory system itself and the economic and political weakness of workers in relation to their bosses.

A century later the mill was in a dilapidated state. The last cloth was woven in 1986 and, unlike

---

START & FINISH: Leeds • DISTANCE: 23 miles / 38km • TOTAL ASCENT: 463m
TERRAIN: Mostly good canal towpath, some roads and one gravel track. Train return. Easy.

Bingley Five Locks

so many mills that were demolished, Salt's Mill was reborn as a cultural and creative space thanks to Jonathan Silver, a Bradford entrepreneur who was every bit as remarkable a character as Titus Salt. He enlisted the help of fellow Bradfordian David Hockney and the mill is now home to the biggest collection of Hockney's work in the world, and all free to view. It's well worth locking up the bike and spending at least an hour wandering around the mill and the rest of the town.

From Saltaire it's back onto the canal for a short ride to Five-Rise Locks in Bingley Ⓓ. Climbing a gradient of 1 in 5, it's the steepest flight of locks in the country. A few miles on in Riddlesden is East Riddlesden Hall Ⓔ (NT, £), a 17th-century manor house with a medieval tithe barn. The house has twice been used as the location for film adaptations of Wuthering Heights.

And it's to the wild, windswept moors that the ride now heads, climbing from Airedale over to Wharfedale. It's a good climb – steep to begin with, easing off as it gets higher. At the top the tarmac ends and it's gravel (Yorkshire grit, if you prefer) across the moor. And not just any old moor but the famous Ilkley Moor. While out rambling, a Yorkshire church choir composed On Ilkla Moor Baht 'at, a dirge-like song that has become Yorkshire's unofficial anthem. The song tells of a man courting his lover on the moor. He is not wearing a hat and catches his death of cold. According to the poet Ian McMillan, who loves the song, it's "a song of renewal and regeneration, as a hymn of praise to the cycle of life and of keeping your hat on whenever you venture across the front step". A recent version commissioned by the Yorkshire Tourist Board has Brian Blessed rapping over breakbeats by the Grimethorpe Colliery Band.

The song is not the only work of art created up here among the heather and gorse. On the moorland ridge, on the track between the two communications masts and the summit trig point, are the Puddle Stones. They are another of the Stanza Stones which feature poems by Yorkshireman Simon Armitage, the current Poet Laureate Ⓕ. Rombalds Moor, of which Ilkley Moor is just a part, has one of the densest concentrations of prehistoric rock carvings in Britain, with more than 400 examples, believed to be between four and five thousand years old. One of them, the Badger Stone Ⓖ, can be found on the way down – turn right onto a rough track for 500 yards.

At the foot of the hill is Ilkley, a well-heeled Victorian spa town that hosts an annual literary festival. It is possible to ride back to Leeds starting out on the famous Cow and Calf hill climb, but the roads on the north-eastern outskirts of the city aren't the nicest on a bike so I suggest taking the train, which will give you just enough time to apply for a Yorkshire passport, should you be so moved.

PUBS & PIT STOPS

TINY TEA ROOM, Rodley LS13 1NF (07710 020791) Cute canal-side stop for a cuppa.

TOBY'S TEA ROOM, Dobson Lock, Esholt BD10 0PY (07817 974926) Coffee and snacks beside the canal.

SALTS DINER, Saltaire BD18 3LA (01274 530533) Big, bustling eatery in Salt's Mill with an inventive, veggie-friendly menu.

CAFÉ IN TO THE OPERA, Saltaire BD18 3LA (01274 531185) Smaller café in Salt's Mill with site-specific murals by David Hockney, fish a speciality.

FIVE RISE LOCKS CAFÉ, Bingley BD16 4DS (01274 569664) Café by the famous locks, breakfasts and light lunches.

N J HOLMES, Riddlesden BD20 5EP (01535 691019) A gem of a traditional greengrocer's from back in the day.

THE COMMUTE, Ilkley LS29 8DS (07888 942007) Cycle café serving breakfast, toasties and damn fine coffee. Workshop and bike bits for sale.

WHITELOCK'S ALE HOUSE, Leeds LS1 6HB (0113 245 3950) Close to the railway station, with a grand Victorian interior that's little changed.

BIKE SHOPS: Cycle Republic, 12-14 Infirmary St, Leeds LS1 2JP (0113 245 3314); All Terrain Cycles, Salt's Mill BD17 7EH (01274 588488) bike hire available; The Commute, Ilkley (see listing above).

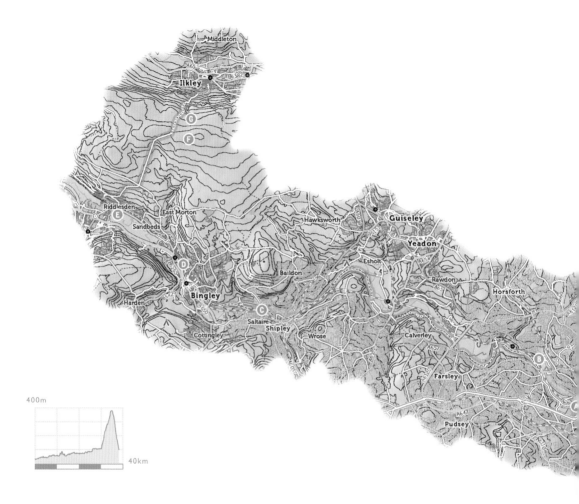

400m

40km

Leeds & Liverpool Canal

Saltaire

Leeds

Salt's Mill

WUTHERING HEIGHTS

Old ways across the wild moors that captivated writers from
the Brontë sisters to Ted Hughes and Sylvia Plath

———

Before the railway came to the South Pennines, before the canals and before the turnpike, there were packhorses. Salt, milk, coal and lime were carried over the Pennines by packhorses as they could negotiate slopes too steep for wheeled vehicles. The convoys consisted of 30-40 pack ponies led in single file by a few men. Many packhorse trails in the Upper Calder Valley owe their existence to weaving, which began a cottage industry. Farmers and their families living on small, often isolated, homesteads would spin the wool from their sheep, and weave it at home on a hand loom. Once the family was clothed, the farmer would tramp to market across the hills with the surplus cloth slung over his back. If he was lucky, he'd have a pony or horse to take the weight. As the industry expanded, weavers grouped together into settlements connected by these hoof-friendly trails.

The routes tended to follow routes along the sides and shoulders of the valleys, avoiding the marshy and overgrown valley bottoms. They went 'over the top' across the moors only when they had to. Many packhorse trails still exist today. Some have been resurfaced in asphalt, some still feature the hefty, hoof-worn blocks of stone painstakingly placed to give the heavily laden animals maximum traction. They are a big part of what makes the Upper Calder Valley such a great place for mountain biking. This route is mostly on road but fits in just enough packhorse trail action to give a sense of how people got around all those years ago.

The ride starts in Hebden Bridge, one of the new towns that grew up as cloth mills put the hand weavers out of business. Before the mills came, Hebden Bridge was just the hamlet by the bridge where the packhorse trains crossed the river. The bigger settlement was up the hill at Heptonstall. Connecting the two is a fearsome cobbled lane known as The Buttress, the venue of an annual cycling hill climb competition (there's a gentler way up via Heptonstall Road if you prefer). Either way, you'll want a breather at Heptonstall and there's plenty to see here Ⓐ. The old church is now an eerie, roofless ruin and in the churchyard are the graves of David Hartley, king of the Cragg Vale Coiners (See Ride No. 25) and Sylvia Plath, the American writer whose husband Ted Hughes hailed from down the valley in Mytholmroyd. Also worth a look is the octagonal Methodist chapel – its roof carried across the moors by packhorses – and the village museum, containing a re-creation of a weaver's cottage, clog-making equipment and coins and counterfeiting moulds from the time of the Hartley gang (free entry, open weekends and bank holidays, March to October).

Above Heptonstall it's up the flank of the valley onto the wastes of Widdop Moor where, in

START & FINISH: Hebden Bridge • DISTANCE: 34 miles / 55km • TOTAL ASCENT: 1162m
TERRAIN: Mostly roads, 2 miles of off-road track. Challenging.

Hebden Bridge

Heptonstall churchyard

the words of Sylvia Plath, "the wind pours by like destiny, bending everything in one direction". On the descent into Trawden look out for Clarion House, now a private home but formerly the club house of the Colne Clarion, a local socialist cycling club Ⓑ. Clarion Houses were once to be found all over the north-west (the last surviving one is across the valley on Pendle Hill, see Ride No. 28). A few miles past Trawden is a lovely off-road interlude following the route of a packhorse trail through Wycoller Ⓒ. There are three ancient bridges: the arched packhorse bridge, the primitive clapper bridge and, a quarter of a mile upstream, the even more primitive clam bridge, made from a single slab of gritstone. Historians argue about their ages; one theory is that they all date from the 16th century, when stonemasons who became unemployed after the dissolution of

the monasteries roamed the country in search of work. The ruins of Wycoller Hall are believed to be the inspiration for Ferndean Manor in Charlotte Brontë's *Jane Eyre* and it seems certain the Brontë sisters would have come this way themselves, from their home over the hill in Haworth.

From here the ride plunges headlong into Brontë country. No place in Britain has chosen to associate itself so doggedly with a single aspect of its history than the town of Haworth has with the Brontë family. It's overkill at times, yet to walk up through the gloomy churchyard to the gate of the parsonage where Charlotte, Emily and Anne lived their short but creatively prodigious lives, it is hard not to be moved. Haworth was a busy mill town like Hebden Bridge, with a notorious reputation for poverty and squalor (the average life expectancy of its residents was 25, and disease was rife, possibly due to the location of the churchyard at the top of the town and the resulting run off from all the rotting corpses into the water supply – yum!) The parsonage is preserved as a museum (Ⓓ £) and beyond it are the moors whose stark beauty and wildness gave Emily Brontë the dramatic inspiration for *Wuthering Heights*. To sample that wildness, there's a rough stuff short cut along the old packhorse route to Hebden Bridge Ⓔ. It's called Stairs Lane and the unsurfaced part of the track is only 1½ miles long, but it is steep and very rough so an off-road-capable bike or a sense of adventure is essential. It passes within two miles of the ruins of Top Withens, the most likely inspiration for the remote moorland farmhouse of *Wuthering Heights*.

If sticking to the road, the route climbs through Oxenhope to Cold Edge (look out for some of the old cobblestones that are emerging from under the tarmac). The packhorse trail back to Hebden Bridge is via Midgely and passes a couple of really good country pubs perfect for a sundowner.

PUBS & PIT STOPS

WHITE LION INN, Heptonstall HX7 7NB (01422 842027) Too early for a drink, but this historic pub has some good Coiners relics. Rooms.

PACK HORSE INN, Widdop HX7 7AT (01422 842803) 17th-century country inn with rooms in a wild, wind-blown setting.

TRAWDEN COMMUNITY SHOP, Trawden BB8 8RZ (01282 869417) Superior village shop for picnic fixings.

PONDEN MILL, near Haworth BD22 0HP (01535 643923) Chilled-out café and B&B in a large Georgian cotton mill. Riverside camping.

Plenty of choice in Haworth: local Timothy Taylor beers at **THE FLEECE INN** (BD22 8DA, 01535 642172) also pub grub, rooms; **APOTHECARY GUEST HOUSE** (BD22 8DP, 01535 643642) is a friendly, good value B&B; great fish and chips at **BETTY SAMPSON'S** on Changegate (BD22 8DY, 01535 642336); the **HAWORTH STEAM BREWERY** (BD22 8DP, 01535 646059) serves food and drink all day.

CAT I'TH WELL, Wainstalls Lane, Halifax HX2 7TR (01422 244841) Quintessential country pub with great views down the valley.

BOB'S TEAROOM AND GARDENS, Jerusalem Lane, Halifax HX2 6XB (01422 884354) Friendly garden tea room with substantial cakes.

HARE AND HOUNDS, Wadsworth HX7 8TN (01422 842671) Stone-built pub above Hebden Bridge, Timothy Taylor on the handpumps. Pub grub, rooms.

OLD CHAMBER, Hebden Bridge HX7 6JG (07814 321606) Small, rustic campsite with good facilities and amazing views.

Plenty of choice in Hebden Bridge for post-ride refreshments including **CALAN'S** micropub (HX7 8EX, 07421 768511) with a sunny courtyard; **OLD GATE** (HX7 8JP, 01422 843993) for craft ales and hearty, good-value food and **CHAPTER 17** (HX7 6EU, 01422 648240) for tasty brunches and gourmet suppers.

BIKE SHOPS: Blazing Saddles, Hebden Bridge HX7 8UQ (01422 844435). Hebden Bridge Visitor Centre HX7 8AD (01422 843831) has five e-bikes for hire at reasonable rates.

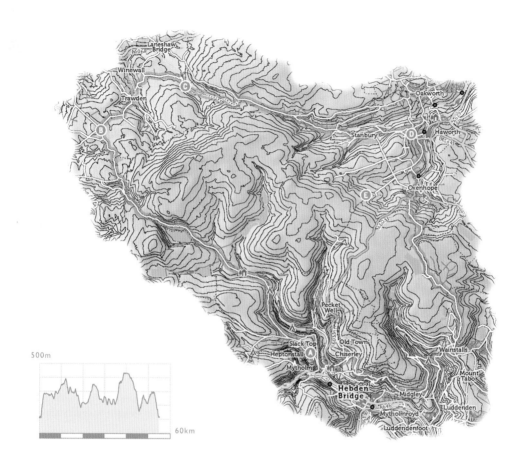

500m

60km

Widdop Moor

Haworth

Wycoller

Oats Royd Mill

A CALDER CAPER

A short route in the Upper Calder Valley taking in the Pennine watershed and the stark landscape of Blackstone Edge

———

Somehow, and nobody knows exactly how, Hebden Bridge went from listless mill town in the late-1960s to become the arty, free-thinking, LGBTQ+-friendly, tech-savvy, hipster capital of the South Pennines. Notwithstanding all the well-groomed beards, the widespread availability of craft ales and the occasional waft of patchouli, it's a pretty good place to live, as confirmed by eye-watering property prices paid by the growing number of commuters to Manchester, Bradford and Leeds.

The ride begins by heading west from here on the Rochdale Canal towards Todmorden. There's a cheerful local rivalry between these two groovy little former mill towns. Todmorden, 'Tod' for short, is a bit rougher around the edges than Hebden Bridge but has a strong claim to be the most green-fingered town in Britain. Its Incredible Edible urban gardening project has seen little plots of land all around the town turned over to growing fruit, vegetables, herbs and bee-friendly flowers. The produce is all free for all to pick and enjoy. This model of urban gardening has been emulated in dozens of towns and cities up and down the country. All around town the word KINDNESS is spelled out in bold white letters, Todmorden's version of the Hollywood sign.

The canal towpath, which is good as far as Todmorden, becomes a bit rougher later. But it's still preferable to the alternative road route proposed by Sustrans (NCR 66). The canal was opened in 1804 as the main highway of commerce between Yorkshire and Lancashire until the first trans-Pennine railway opened in 1840. Engineered by George Stephenson, the 'father of the railways', the rail line negotiates the summit pass through a 1½-mile long tunnel cut by an army of men and boys armed only with hand tools and candles, 28 men of whom were killed by accidents.

In 1985 a train carrying a million litres of petrol derailed in mid-tunnel and caught fire. The inferno in the tunnel briefly turned the hill into a volcano as fire shot out of the ventilation shafts to a height of 50 metres. Amazingly, nobody was hurt and the tunnel was repaired. Above the tunnel, the Pennine watershed is marked by a cast-iron bench and a poem by Barnsley poet Andrew McMillan Ⓐ.

At Littleborough the route leaves the canal and heads uphill on what is undoubtedly an ancient way across the Pennines. Cutting tools made from flint, a stone which doesn't occur naturally in West Yorkshire, have been found here and dated to 10,000 years ago. A bridleway branching off to the right just after the junction with the A58 has flummoxed archaeologists. Roman road, turnpike,

---

START & FINISH: Hebden Bridge • DISTANCE: 24 miles / 38km • TOTAL ASCENT: 471m
TERRAIN: Canal towpath, roads, lanes and a short section of good gravel track. Easy.

quarry tramway? A little way higher up there are a couple of 19th-century milestones to spot. Daniel Defoe came this way on his tours of the North and nearly came to grief in an August snowstorm. No wonder he described Blackstone Edge as 'the Andes of England'.

At the top is a brief but sublime detour on a track along the top of the escarpment beside the reservoir. The glass and steel towers of Manchester are clearly visible, and on a fine day you can see the mountains of North Wales. The bare hills, the pylons leading off into the distance, the cold, dark reservoirs with their wind-blown wavelets, wind-hewn rocks and abandoned quarry workings make it a perfect – and popular – location for a moody album cover or fashion shoot. In all this solitude it is hard to imagine the scene in 1846 when 30,000 people from nearby industrial towns

gathered here under the Chartist banner to talk radicalism, political reform and workers' rights. The event is commemorated every year with a walk and a picnic where radical songs are sung.

Visible from the track is a slab of weather-sculpted millstone grit, the size of a house. It is part the old Cow's Mouth quarry works Ⓑ. On it is carved a poem by Simon Armitage entitled 'Rain' – an appropriate choice of subject given the location. Appointed Poet Laureate in 2019, Armitage hails from Marsden, just a few miles across the moor. There are five other 'Stanza Stones', one of which can be found on Ride No. 23.

The route turns right at the second of a series of reservoirs, but if you carry straight on for 2½ miles on an increasingly uneven track you will eventually reach Gaddings Dam Ⓒ. It has a small patch of golden sand that made national newspaper headlines as England's highest beach, accompanied by the inevitable photos of bikini-clad sun worshippers soaking up the rays.

The reservoirs were built to supply water to operate the locks in the canal, and gravity is also on hand to take you back to the Calder Valley. The Blackstone Edge road (B6138) is the longest continuous descent in England: five miles long, with a drop of almost 300 metres. It passes the village of Cragg Vale, the base of the infamous gang of Coiners who, in the late-18th century, supplemented meagre earnings from weaving by shaving the edges off coins and smelting the shavings to make counterfeit coins. So big was

their 'yellow trade' that its effect on the money supply spooked the Treasury. The law caught up with them in the end, and their leader "King" David Hartley was hanged at York (his grave is in Heptonstall churchyard, Ride No. 24). The story, the landscape and the brutality of life in those times are brilliantly conjured in visceral detail by local author Benjamin Myers in his novel *The Gallows Pole*. Though the longest descent in England has an obvious appeal, more rewarding in terms of great views and quiet lanes is the route via Sykes Gate, Holly Hall Lane and Long Causeway. Back in the Calder Valley at Mytholmroyd, NCR 68 follows the river back to Hebden Bridge.

PUBS & PIT STOPS

Lots to choose from in Todmorden: **GOLDEN LION** (OL14 6LZ, 01706 816333) is a big quayside pub with Thai food and a good live music scene; **KAVA KAFE** (OL14 7LA, 01706 810880) is a justly popular vege and vegan café by the canal; **YAKUMAMA** (OL14 7LA, 07809 646062) is a zesty vegetarian cantina in the fabulous old co-op shop; **THE PUB** (OL14 5AJ, 01706 812145) and **THE ALEHOUSE** (OL14 5EY, 07407 747956) are ace micropubs.

THE WHITE HOUSE, Blackstone Edge OL15 0LG (01706 378456) Much-extended and modernised old coaching inn by the reservoirs. Well-kept real ales.

THE HINCHLIFFE ARMS, Cragg Vale HX7 5TA (01422 883256) Foodies flock to Rob Owen Jones's local and seasonal dishes at very reasonable prices. Requires a short cut via Cragg Vale.

Plenty of choice in Hebden Bridge for post-ride refreshments including **CALAN'S** micropub (HX7 8EX, 07421 768511) with a sunny courtyard; **OLD GATE** (HX7 8JP, 01422 843993) for craft ales and hearty, good-value food and **CHAPTER 17** (HX7 6EU, 01422 648240) for tasty brunches and gourmet suppers.

BIKE SHOPS: Blazing Saddles, Hebden Bridge HX7 8UQ (01422 844435). Hebden Bridge Visitor Centre HX7 8AD (01422 843831) has five e-bikes for hire at reasonable rates.

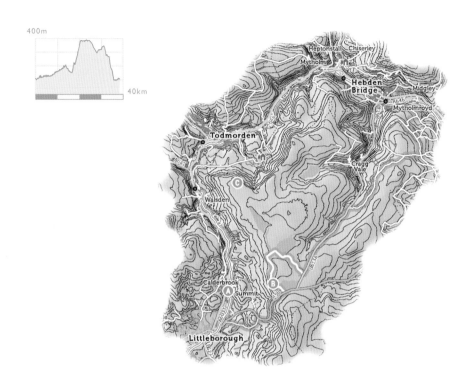

400m

40km

Todmorden

Hebden Bridge

The Rain Stone

HAMMER AND CHISEL

Art abounds in this circuit of the gently rolling landscape
of the South Yorkshire Coalfield

———

"All my early memories are of forms and shapes and textures. Moving through and over the West Riding landscape with my father in his car, the hills were sculptures; the roads defined the form. Above all, there was the sensation of moving physically over the contours of fulnesses and concavities, through hollows and over peaks – feeling, touching, seeing, through mind and hand and eye. This sensation has never left me. I, the sculptor, am the landscape." That's how sculptor Barbara Hepworth recalls growing up in Wakefield in the first decades of the 20th century. There's a sculptural and architectural theme to this ride around the gently rolling countryside between Wakefield and Barnsley, just to the east of the Pennines.

Heading south out of the city centre, the ride passes the Hepworth Gallery, which sits astride a bend in the River Calder. The striking building is a cast concrete counterpoint to the 14th-century chantry bridge complete with chapel, a little downstream. The gallery spaces are airy and spacious, filled with Hepworth's work, mostly prototypes and full-size plaster mock-ups of stone and bronze sculptures as well as her archive and a selection of her working tackle. Heading out of the city, the route takes in sections of the Wakefield Wheel, a 37-mile circular cycle route devised by the local volunteer cycling group, mostly on traffic-free, off-road paths.

Most of the ride is in the South Yorkshire Coalfield. The mines are all closed now, their winding gear used for scrap metal, the spoil tips grassed over. A way of life erased in just a few years. But down there, the earth remains honeycombed with the shafts and tunnels dug by generations of Yorkshire miners.

A long grind of a climb leads to Woolley Edge Ⓐ from where there's a big view west to Emley Moor transmitting station. At 330m high, it's the tallest free-standing structure in Britain, a full 20m higher than The Shard in London. It's made of reinforced concrete and its shapely, curved sides are reminiscent of Berlin's iconic TV Tower, though sadly there's no bar and viewing area at the top.

It's always a pleasure to ride over a motorway on a bike, and this crossing of the M1 is no exception. Henry Moore once said "Sculpture is an art of the open air... I would rather have a piece of my sculpture put in a landscape, almost any landscape, than in, or on, the most beautiful building I know." He'd love the Yorkshire Sculpture Park Ⓑ. A bonus of arriving by bike is that there's no entry fee. There are dozens of works including by Moore, Hepworth, Elisabeth Frink, Eduardo Paolozzi, Andy Goldsworthy, Ai Weiwei, Damien Hirst and more. As well as

---

START & FINISH: Wakefield • DISTANCE: 41 miles / 66km • TOTAL ASCENT: 854m
TERRAIN: Mostly roads and lanes with a few sections of unsurfaced cycleway. Moderate.

Cannon Hall

open-air exhibits there are gallery and installation spaces and a great café in the visitor centre. It would be easy to spend a whole day here.

An unsurfaced bridleway runs through the park to the Cascade Bridge and out the other side. Back on the lanes, there's a gradual climb west to the wind farm on Royd Moor Ⓒ. This is the edge of the Pennines. A railway once crossed the high moor, reducing the journey between Manchester and Sheffield from eight days by canal or two days by packhorse, to a little over an hour. The Woodhead line closed in 1981 and much of the trackbed now forms part of the Trans Pennine Trail long-distance cycling and walking route, though there is talk of reopening the line one day.

Penistone is the most westerly and most rural of Barnsley's outlying villages, and has a distinctly Pennine feel. Rather than coal, it was farming and then the railway that built the town. From here the route turns east towards Wakefield and back into coal country. A few miles on is Cannon Hall, a Georgian mansion built by the Spencer-Stanhope family who made a fortune in the local iron industry but also dabbled in the transatlantic slave trade. It's now owned by Barnsley Council and run as a country park and museum with a particular emphasis on ceramics and glassware Ⓓ (free entry). The route follows a path through the parkland to the estate village of Cawthorne. The highlight here is the village museum. It's a real cabinet of curiosities whose exhibits include the usual collection of butterflies, moths, birds' eggs and fossils, but also a stuffed cheetah, a two-headed lamb, a cobra in combat with a mongoose, a mantrap, and a figure of John Wesley made from the backbone of a whale. The museum was set up with the help of a Pre-Raphaelite group of artists and is the only survivor of John Ruskin's vision of a nationwide network of village museums.

In Cawthorne churchyard there is a new memorial to mark the previously unmarked graves of six men and boys who were among ten who were killed in the nearby Norcroft colliery disaster in 1821. Two miles away in Silkstone churchyard are buried the bodies of 26 children, aged between 7 and 17, who were drowned underground in the Huskar pit disaster in 1838. Bone and blood is the price of coal, as the ballad goes.

There's a train bailout option at Darton Ⓔ, otherwise it's a traverse of the Barnsley-Wakefield borderlands before picking up the Trans Pennine Trail / NCR 67 and then the Wakefield Wheel for a largely traffic-free return to the city, crossing back over the river on the chantry bridge.

PUBS & PIT STOPS

THE HEPWORTH CAFÉ, Wakefield WF1 5AW (01924 247371) Bright, airy bistro-café in the Hepworth Wakefield with artful cooking and great coffee.

YSP CAFÉ, Yorkshire Sculpture Park, West Bretton WF4 4LG (01924 832631) Gallery café serving good food with views across the parkland.

ARTHOUSE CAFÉ & DELI, Penistone S36 6AR (01226 765080) Small café serving decent light meals and cakes.

THE HUNTSMAN, Thurlstone S36 9QW (01226 764892) Trad village pub serving a good range of real ales and pies from local producers.

PAVILION CAFÉ, Cannon Hall S75 4AT (01226 792777) Small café serving sandwiches, soups, cakes and pastries, outside seating.

In Cawthorne, **THE SPENCER ARMS** (S75 4HL, 01226 792795) is a popular gastropub. **BEATSON HOUSE** (S75 4HR, 01226 791245) is renowned for its Barnsley chops and Sunday lunches, booking essential. The **VILLAGE STORES** (S75 4HR, 01226 792829) is a tea room for lighter bites.

THE KINGS ARMS, Heath Common WF1 5SE (01924 377527) A glorious relic of bygone times, a must-visit for serious pub aficionados. Gas-lit dining room.

BIKE SHOPS: Cycle Technology, Wakefield WF1 5PE (01924 311234). Cycle Penistone, Penistone S36 6DT (01226 872310) Great local bike shop with a full range of bikes and e-bikes for hire.

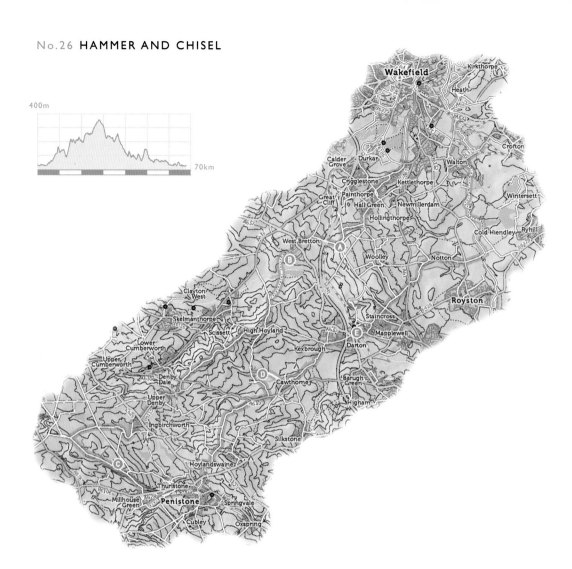

400m

70km

The Hepworth Wakefield

Chantry Bridge

Yorkshire Sculpture Park

Royd Moor wind farm

WHERE THERE'S MUCK

A rough stuff excursion taking in riverside paths,
old railway lines and forest trails north of Sheffield

———

Sheffield is the southernmost outpost of the North. The River Sheaf, which gives the city its name, formed the old border between the Anglo-Saxon kingdoms of Northumbria and Mercia. It is built on hills that turn the city centre into a citadel and help define the city's neighbourhoods. There is dazzling architecture, from serene Georgian to ornate Victorian to international modernist, municipal brutalist, cacophonous postmodern and 21st-century abstract. There are rivers, canals, railways, trams and a network of cycling infrastructure that seems to get better every year. As a city of making and industry it has a long pedigree. Chaucer name-checks Sheffield knives in *The Canterbury Tales*, and five centuries later Sheffield metallurgists invented stainless steel. The city is still in the steel business but long-gone is the legion of 'little mesters' who put the words 'Made in Sheffield' into cutlery drawers around the world. You can learn all about them, and much more, at the brilliant Kelham Island Industrial Museum near the end of the ride.

The ride starts out heading east along the River Don, following the Five Weirs Walk. The riverside path is traffic-free with the exception of a short diversion around sprawling Forgemasters, Europe's largest steel foundry Ⓐ. It makes parts for power stations, oil rigs, pipelines and other heavy engineering uses and claims the record for

making the largest single piece of steel, weighing a staggering 325 tonnes.

As recently as the early 1980s steelworks lined the Don all the way to Rotherham. One of those sites is now home to Meadowhall, a gigantic shopping mall. It's the same story of replacement right across South Yorkshire as mining and steel-making have given way to retail parks, distribution centres and warehouses. Rotherham has never escaped Sheffield's shadow and hasn't helped itself lately by demolishing many of its best buildings. The town is home to Planet X, the iconoclastic bicycle company that pioneered online sales and no-nonsense prices. To avoid Rotherham's busy main roads the route heads off-road past the town's allotments and across fields, suddenly emerging into an English Arcadia, with added fly-tipping.

Beyond Greasbrough is the realm of the Earls Fitzwilliam. They were politically active Yorkshire gentry with landholdings that straddled the Barnsley coal seam, a three-metre-thick layer that produced half the output of the entire South Yorkshire Coalfield. Wentworth Woodhouse, the family seat, is the biggest privately owned home in Britain with a room for every day of the year and a frontage twice the length of Buckingham Palace Ⓓ. All paid for by the toil of thousands of men and boys deep underground. Politically, the family was on the liberal side of things and were said to be kindly employers, at

---

START & FINISH: Sheffield • DISTANCE: 35 miles / 57km • TOTAL ASCENT: 557m
TERRAIN: Canal towpath, roads, lanes and off-road tracks. Moderate.

Wentworth

least by the measure of the times. During the general strike of 1926, the seventh Earl, by now among the richest men in Britain, kept his workers fed for their eight months without pay and taught some of them to play polo on pit ponies on his front lawn.

Even so, his sister, Lady Mabel, couldn't abide the rank injustice of it all and became a committed socialist who campaigned for workers' education and votes for women. For drama, intrigue, scandal and tragedy the Fitzwilliam family saga puts Downton Abbey in the shade. The lurid story of wealth and privilege built on lives of grinding hardship is told in compelling style by Catherine Bailey in her bestseller *Black Diamonds*. Next in line to the Fitzwilliam fortune is Helena Rees-Mogg, wife of the Conservative politician Jacob Rees-Mogg.

The route picks a way to the estate village of Wentworth along the way passing the Hoober Stand Ⓑ and the Needle's Eye Ⓒ, two of a handful of follies built as displays of power and prestige. Down the hill is Elsecar, the site of a Fitzwilliam colliery and ironworks Ⓔ. It's now an industrial heritage centre with a working Newcomen engine used to pump the water out from the mines.

Next door to Elsecar is Hoyland, a former pit village and home of the late Barry Hines. Hines 1968 novel *A Kestrel for a Knave* was adapted for film by director Ken Loach. A landmark in British cinema, Kes was filmed in and around Hoyland with untrained local people cast in the main roles. On the way out of Hoyland, the route passes the crumbling ruins of Tankersley Old Hall where Billy Casper first finds the kestrel Kes Ⓕ. Hines's *The Price of Coal*, a novel and two-part BBC TV drama also directed by Loach, is a faithful and deeply affectionate portrait of a South Yorkshire coal mining community.

After a great track across farm fields the route follows the Trans Pennine Trail onto the first Sheffield to Manchester railway line, now a cycling and walking path. Off the route and down the hill by the River Don is Wortley Top Forge, a water-powered iron forge now run as an industrial museum Ⓖ (open Sundays and bank holidays from Easter to October). It gives a sense of the small-scale beginnings of the Industrial Revolution, a massive contrast with high-tech Forgemasters passed earlier in the ride.

A good gravel trail leads through steep-sided Wharncliffe Woods to Oughtibridge, a mill town-turned-leafy commuter village, followed by a track through Beeley Wood beside the River Don. Re-entry into Sheffield comes as a shock with its sprawl of retail parks and industrial estates along the busy A61. Fortunately, there's a separate cycle path and it's briefly back across the Don for the last stretch along Club Mill Lane which, at time of writing, is home to an encampment of New Age travellers Ⓗ. They moved here after the council evicted them from a nearby site where they had lived peacefully for fifteen years. Crossing the Don at Ball Bridge it's onto Kelham Island Ⓘ and back into the city centre.

PUBS & PIT STOPS

CUTLERS' ARMS, Rotherham S60 1BQ (01709 382581) Big, grand Edwardian boozer that escaped Rotherham's wrecking ball.

GEORGE & DRAGON, Wentworth S62 7TN (01226 742440) Plenty of Fitzwilliamiana in this village pub with a pie-centric food menu.

BRAMBLES TEA ROOM, Elsecar S74 8HJ (01226 741915) Good-value bites in this trad tea room in the Elsecar Heritage Centre.

CASPERS, Hoyland Common S74 0NT (01226 742144) Off-route, but Kes fans will want to visit the chippy where Billy Casper bought the fateful fish and chips.

THE WORTLEY ARMS, Wortley S35 7DB (0114 288 8749) Coaching inn built in 1753, plenty of interesting old features. Pies and pub grub.

COUNTESS TEA ROOM, Wortley S35 7DB (0114 327 4090) Classic tea room fare: breakfasts, toasties, jacket potatoes and plenty of cakes.

TRAVELLERS REST, Oughtibridge S35 0GY (0114 286 2221) Samuel Smith's winning formula of a nice old pub interior and good, cheap beer.

THE GARDENER'S REST, Sheffield S3 8AT (0114 272 4978) This community-run pub is a Neepsend landmark. Bar billiards, no food.

THE FAT CAT, Sheffield S3 8SA (0114 249 4801) Friendly and authentic neighbourhood boozer. Real ales and simple, good-value food.

THE RIVERSIDE, Kelham, Sheffield S3 8EN (0114 272 4640) Open all day, serving vege-friendly bistro food and craft beer overlooking the river.

BIKE SHOP: Russell's Bicycle Shed S1 2BP (0114 273 0539) Big bike shop by the train station, good-value hire bikes. Another branch in Neepsend S3 8BX (0114 327 1970).

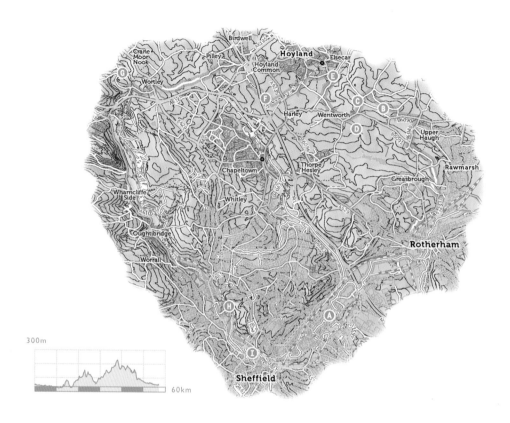

300m

60km

Hoober Stand

Wentworth

Kelham Island

LANCASHIRE

THE GIANT OF RIBBLESDALE

Around Lancashire's most legendary hill, travelling through the land
of witches, radicals and champion cyclists

———

As mighty, white-topped Mont Ventoux is to sun-kissed Provence, so dark, brooding Pendle Hill is to rain-soaked Lancashire. For each of them, their power of attraction comes from prominence in low-lying country, the way they stand as a constant on the horizon, set apart from their surroundings. Medieval poets and philosophers were drawn to Ventoux. In 1652 the preacher George Fox climbed Pendle Hill where he had a vision of a "great people to be gathered" that led him to found Quakerism.

The ride begins in Clitheroe, a sturdy medieval town with a Norman castle. The town is host to an annual jazz and blues festival, a food festival and, in the past few years, a Cycle Touring Festival. It's a weekend gathering of pedal-powered travellers and adventurers who come to camp out, make merry and share stories. The climb out of Clitheroe starts gently and gets steeper and steeper. The word 'Pendle' already combines two different words for hill – 'Pen' is Celtic, 'hyll' is Old English. Appending the modern English 'hill' makes it a triple tautology and by the time you reach the top at Nick o' Pendle you may want to add a fourth. And this is the easy way up. The steeper side, from Sabden, has featured in the Tour of Britain and in 1988 a young Chris Boardman won the first of four straight national hill climb

titles by setting a course record of 3 minutes and 29 seconds. He rode a fixed wheel with a 60-inch gear and his time hasn't been bettered since.

Sabden grew as an outpost of Lancashire's vast complex of textile mills, and its seven mills employed over 2,000 people. After a stiff climb to the ridge road of Padiham Heights the scene is thoroughly rural. Far below is the linear metropolis of Burnley, Nelson and Colne, at one time the world's biggest producers of cotton cloth. From those mill towns, and from towns all across the industrial North, came cyclists and ramblers looking to escape the stink, the racket and the filth. Dozens of local socialist groups raised funds to set up scores of club houses in the countryside, often under the red and yellow banner of the Clarion Cycling Club. The last of the Clarion houses is on Jinny Lane just beyond Newchurch in Pendle and is going strong, supported by local activists who continue to fight for workers' rights, women's rights, social justice and access to land Ⓐ.

In the early 1930s one local cyclist who worked in a cotton mill in Nelson decided to make a saddlebag to his own specifications. His friends began asking for copies and he started turning them out on a sewing machine in his mother's back bedroom. His name was Wilf Carradice; his hobby quickly grew into a business producing

---

START & FINISH: Clitheroe • DISTANCE: 34 miles / 54km • TOTAL ASCENT: 909m
TERRAIN: All lanes. Moderate.

Sawley Bridge

bicycle luggage and other outdoor kit like tents, sleeping bags and camping stoves. Carradice is still producing cotton canvas cycle luggage in Nelson. Every one of them is hand-stitched and signed by its maker. Nelson is also the birthplace of jelly babies, the soft, sugary sweets beloved of cyclists, which were originally sold by the rather disturbing but very Victorian name of 'Unclaimed Babies'.

Barley is the village most people choose to start an ascent of Pendle Hill, or to take the long-distance trail to Lancaster Castle, following the fateful journey made by a dozen local people to the castle where, in 1612, they were tried for witch-craft. This was a time of political and religious turmoil. England had embraced a Puritan form of Protestantism and the new king imported from Scotland, James I, had narrowly escaped

being blown to bits in a Catholic terrorist attack. The King was paranoid about witches plotting against him. Puritans saw rural Lancashire as a "dark corner of the land", rife with Catholicism and other demonic superstitions. The witch trials gripped the nation, not least because the star witness was a nine-year-old beggar girl whose evidence sent her own mother, brother and sister to the gallows, along with eight others.

Regardless of whether or not witchcraft has ever existed, belief in and fear of witchcraft was undoubtedly real. Village healers or 'cunning women' were a part of everyday life, especially for the poor who couldn't afford to visit a doctor or a lawyer, and some of these healers did invoke magic in their cures. Threats of bewitching also played a part in extortion and protection rackets, and accusations of witchcraft were a way of settling scores between rival families. It seems likely that the victims were framed by investigators looking to curry favour with the King and convicted by judges with an eye on their own advancement.

From Barley the road heads up Pendle Hill on a road right beneath the summit and then down into the village of Downham. It's an estate village owned by the Assheton family since 1558 Ⓑ. The family has sought to minimise the intrusion of the 20th century – there are no modern buildings, no overhead cables, satellite dishes or TV aerials. This makes it a popular location for period films. The only blots on the landscape are the parked cars.

Every bit as lovely as Downham is the lane that rolls east towards Barnoldswick (the lower road via Rimington is not bad either). After you're over the A682, Coal Pit Lane to Gisburn is another cracker: narrow and lined with gnarled, coppiced hedges. It's part of the new Great North Trail, a continuous 825-mile lanes-and-tracks route between the Peak District and the north coast of Scotland.

The return to Clitheroe follows the Ribble downstream on its north bank, with views across to the big hill. Along the way are a few villages with pubs and some good spots for a swim if the river's not in spate: Brungerley Bridge Ⓒ and Edisford Bridge Ⓓ are both popular with locals.

PUBS & PIT STOPS

CLARION HOUSE, Newchurch-in-Pendle BB12 9LL The last of the Clarion Houses. Café open Sundays from 10.30am to 4pm.

CABIN CAFÉ, Barley BB12 9JX (01282 696937) Breakfasts, hot drinks and light meals at this log cabin in the car park.

ASSHETON ARMS, Downham BB7 4BJ (01200 441227) Smart dining pub with rooms and outside seating in beautiful Downham.

THE GARDEN KITCHEN, Holden Clough BB7 4PF (01200 447447) Just off-route, a fantastic café and farm shop in this plant nursery. Open all day.

COACH & HORSES, Bolton-by-Bowland BB7 4NW (01200 447331) Upmarket pub with very good food and plush rooms, onsite brewery.

LOWER BUCK INN, Waddington BB7 3HU (01200 423342) Cosy village inn with B&B and a reputation for good, hearty pub food.

BASHALL BARN FARM SHOP, Bashall BB7 3LQ (01200 428964) Just off-route, a farm shop, bistro and ice cream parlour.

BIKE SHOP: Cycles Recycled, Clitheroe BB7 1PG (01200 442306) Community bike shop with great deals on bike hire including e-bikes.

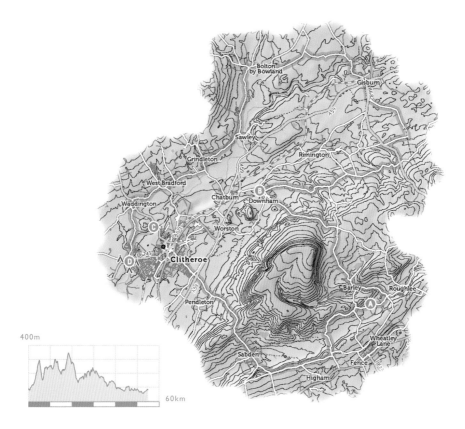

400m

60km

Clarion House

Pendle Hill

TAKE THE HIGH ROAD

Across the Forest of Bowland on a sensational upland gravel track
and back via the highest paved road across the fells

———

The Forest of Bowland is sometimes described as a well-kept secret and it's true that it gets far fewer visitors than its neighbours the Yorkshire Dales and the Lake District. But for the club cyclists of Lancaster, Preston, Blackpool, Burnley and Blackburn, the Bowland Fells are the go-to roads for testing the legs. Bradley Wiggins did his winter training here before becoming the first British winner of the Tour de France and made his home here in a converted barn. The Trough of Bowland is the premier cycling road but is probably too well known to qualify for inclusion in a book about lost lanes.

Instead, this ride takes in one of the best gravel roads in the country, which is genuinely a well-kept cycling secret. Hornby Road is also known as the Salter Fell Track and the Old Salt Road (perhaps for transporting sea salt harvested in Morecambe Bay). Its eastern end was once a Roman road, and in medieval times it must have been a significant packhorse route across the fells. Today it's used by just a few farmers, gamekeepers and grouse-shooting parties. Alfred Wainwright is said to have considered it to be the best moorland walk in Britain. For an upland track that climbs to over 400m, the surface is remarkably good: fine, hard-packed gravel that is quite rideable on 28mm tyres with the exception of a half-mile section

where it is little loose. If you're thoroughly gravel-phobic you can keep to the tarmac throughout by following the classic Trough of Bowland route from Lancaster via Quernmore and Dunsop Bridge, joining the route at Slaidburn. This is quite a long route with a fair amount of climbing; it's perfect for splitting over two days, with an overnight stop in Slaidburn and plenty of time for stops and detours.

From Lancaster the ride begins along the cycleway beside the River Lune as far as Caton. If you're planning to picnic, there's a co-op here where you can buy provisions. Look out for the fish stones: three sandstone steps used in medieval times by local monks to display and sell fish caught from the River Lune Ⓐ. The venerable oak tree that once shaded the site is on its last legs. Here the climbing begins, first up towards the wind farm on Caton Moor. Agonisingly, almost all the hard work is then undone on the steep descent to the River Roeburn and must be repeated on the climb to High Salter Farm. From here it's gravel for the next eight glorious miles.

It's possible that the unfortunate souls from around Pendle Hill were led this way in 1612 to their trial and execution in Lancaster for witch-craft. Then again, the same claim is made for the Trough of Bowland route as well, and they can't

---

START & FINISH: Lancaster • DISTANCE: 51 miles / 82km • TOTAL ASCENT: 1276m
TERRAIN: Lanes, tarmac cycleway and a 5-mile section of gravel track. Challenging.

Hornby Road

both be true. At any rate, to mark the 400th anniversary of the trials, a series of ten waymarkers were installed between Pendle Hill and Lancaster to commemorate the victims. One of them stands on Croasdale Fell, about a mile past the high point of the track, and is inscribed with a poem by Carol Ann Duffy which speaks of the poverty, superstition, misogyny and injustice of the whole tragic affair Ⓑ. For more on the Pendle witch trials see Ride No. 28.

Up here in the solitude of the high fells is the best place to spot a hen harrier, Bowland's iconic bird of prey. The hen harrier clings on here despite habitat loss and persecution by unscrupulous gamekeepers. Grouse shooting is big business in Bowland, and there is a simmering conflict between the big estates and wildlife conservationists. There are also peregrines and merlins. Much

easier to spot than any of those are lapwings, curlews and oystercatchers. You may well hear them before you see them – audio recordings of their distinctive calls are available on the websites of the Forest of Bowland AONB and the RSPB.

It's a relief to be back on the hard road and soon enough you arrive in Slaidburn, for many people the best-looking village in Bowland. Historically in the West Riding of Yorkshire, it's been part of Lancashire since 1974 and there's a pub, a youth hostel, a riverside tea room and an antique but still functional drinking-water tap facing the war memorial. A stop for refreshments is a wise idea as the return route takes in Bowland's highest road. The Cross of Greet climb tops out at 427m and offers big views to the Three Peaks of the Yorkshire Dales. On the way down, and just slightly off-route is the Great Stone of

Fourstones, an elephantine, glacial erratic – a stone transported by an ancient glacier from its place of origin – that serves to mark the border between Lancashire and Yorkshire ©.

It's all downhill beside the densely wooded River Hindburn to Wray, a Bowland village which vies with Slaidburn for loveliness, and then via Hornby, beneath the sandstone battlements of Hornby Castle and over the River Lune floodplain to Gressingham. NCR 69 continues high above the Lune Valley, crossing the river on the Crook O'Lune viaduct Ⓓ where it picks up the Lune Cycleway from the start of the ride for the return journey to Lancaster.

PUBS & PIT STOPS

STATION HOTEL, Caton LA2 9QS (01524 770690) Large, traditional pub with a good choice of cask ales. Pub grub served all day.

CO-OP, Caton LA2 9QW (01524 770269) Last stop for picnic supplies.

HARK TO BOUNTY INN, Slaidburn BB7 3EP (01200 446246) Unfussy 16th-century village pub with rooms serving hearty pub classics.

RIVERBANK TEAROOMS, Slaidburn BB7 3ES (01200 446398) All-day breakfasts, jacket potatoes and the usual tearoom fare.

THE INN AT WHITEWELL, Whitewell BB7 3AT (01200 448222) A few miles off-route but nowhere better for an overnight stay in Bowland.

YHA SLAIDBURN, Slaidburn BB7 3ER (0345 371 9343) Once the Black Bull pub, this tiny hostel is one of the YHA's oldest.

GEORGE & DRAGON, Wray LA2 8QG (01524 221403) Very trad village pub, food served, outside seating.

BRIDGE HOUSE FARM TEA ROOM, LA2 8QP (01524 237775) Bike-friendly tea rooms, food served all day.

HORNBY TEA ROOMS, Hornby LA2 8JR (01524 221237) Small café, shop and post office. Home-made food served all day.

WOODIE'S, near Halton LA2 6PA (07967 121809) Snack kiosk by the Crook O'Lune viewpoint.

BIKE SHOP: On Yer Bike Cycles, Lancaster LA1 3NY (01524 60554) Bike shop just off the Lune River path. Full range of hire bikes and e-bikes available.

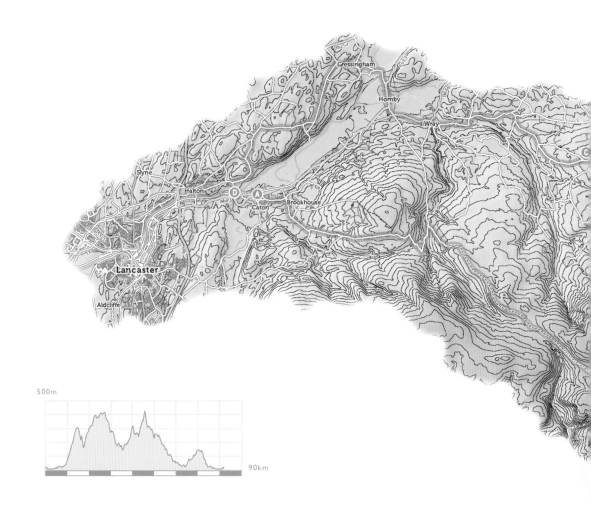

Great Stone of Fourstones

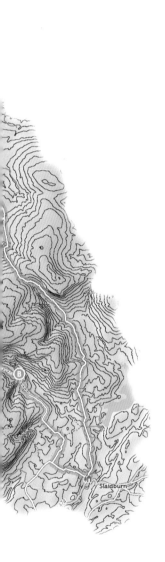

Slaidburn

Slaidburn

BRIEF ENCOUNTER

Through the limestone country of the north Lancashire coast to foodie
Cartmel and the peaceful backwoods of the Winster Valley

———

In David Lean's film *Brief Encounter* Carnforth Station is more than just a stage set for Noël Coward's story of an intense but ultimately doomed love affair. It is an essential player in the story, advancing the action, creating moments of tension and urgency. The steam trains, which convey so much emotion in the film, are long gone and the station is no longer on the mainline, but the refreshment room, the big clock and the ramps up to the platforms are all still there. Rescued from dereliction by volunteers, the station has become a place of pilgrimage for film buffs, and there are exhibition rooms where the film is shown on a loop alongside displays about life in the 1940s, the works of David Lean and assorted railway ephemera.

Though it's possible that while cycling you'll get a speck of grit in your eye and have it removed by a dashing stranger, the principal brief encounter on the ride is with the southernmost tip of the Lake District National Park. You could, of course, take the train from Carnforth but that would miss out on the first eight miles of the ride through the low limestone hills, ancient woodland, salt marshes and estuarine coast of Silverdale and Arnside. This is where the pale limestone block of the Yorkshire Dales comes to an abrupt end at Morecambe Bay to the west and the dark mudstones and slates of the Lake District to the north. Though the lanes are nice enough, the best of the area requires a short detour on foot to spots like Jack Scout and Jenny Brown's Point Ⓐ (just south of Silverdale) and The Cove Ⓑ (immediately west of Silverdale). They are well signposted from the road.

The biggest obstacle to cycling around Morecambe Bay is the lack of crossings of the rivers that flow into it. There are no road bridges, and for centuries people used to make the perilous journey on foot across the shifting sands. In medieval times the responsibility for shepherding them across fell to the monks of Cartmel Priory and later to the crown. The monarch continues to appoint an official Guide to the Sands who gets the use of a cottage at Kents Bank and a stipend of £15 a year. Eventually the railway came and the low-slung Kent Viaduct was built across the mouth of the river. It opened in 1887, on the eve of the first great bicycle boom, and it's a shame nobody had thought to build a walking and cycling path alongside. Thus it's necessary to hop on the train for the six-minute crossing. The trains go every hour, so check the timetables and be ready to charm the conductor if there are more bikes than usual.

Facing Arnside from across the water is Grange-over-Sands, a fishing village that the railway transformed into a seaside resort. It retains a faded Edwardian elegance with orna-

---

START & FINISH: Carnforth • DISTANCE: 43 miles / 69km • TOTAL ASCENT: 816m
TERRAIN: Lanes, one short train link. Moderate.

Cartmel

mental gardens that bask in the Gulf Stream and summer sunshine. Over the hill is Cartmel, a pretty village with a colourful history. It all began when land was gifted to the monks of Lindisfarne in 674. Five centuries later the Normans established an Augustinian priory endowed with lands between the rivers Leven and Winster. Though wealthy, the priory was not always well run. The Pope dismissed one prior who was running the place as a business, doing very little praying and too much drinking. Later, Cartmel monks were leading figures in the Pilgrimage of Grace, a northern revolt against Henry VIII and the dissolution of the monasteries. The revolt failed and those involved were sentenced to a traitor's death of being hung, drawn and quartered. Most of the priory was demolished but local people begged for the church to be spared. It's well worth a look around what must be one of the biggest village churches in the country.

Besides coming to Cartmel to pray, people come to take a punt on the horse racing (the main meet is over the Whitsun weekend), to drink in its pubs, and perhaps most of all, to eat. In 1990 the owners of the village shop started making a few ready meals for passing tourists. Their sticky toffee pudding was a hit and the business has mushroomed into an operation that turns out more than a million of the dense, sweet and intensely moreish desserts a year. At the other end of the sophistication league is L'Enclume which has two Michelin stars and regularly tops lists of the best restaurants in Britain. For a gourmet picnic supplies there is an excellent cheese shop, a sourdough bakery, a wine merchant and a micro-brewery.

The next section of the ride shows how easy it is to get off the tourist trail in the Lakes. It begins with a climb up Cartmel Fell then a joyous descent to Bowland Bridge ©. A perfect lost lane via Witherslack begins the journey back to Carnforth. The road passes beneath the limestone cliffs of Whitbarrow which were built up beneath a tropical sea and sculpted into their present shape during the last ice age ⓓ.

The remainder of the ride passes a string of historic manor houses and their estates. Levens Hall is famous for its gardens which feature the world's oldest topiary, dating back to the 1690s Ⓔ (£). Next, the route runs through the deer park of Dallam Tower Ⓕ. After a lane through some dense woodland straight out of Tim Burton's *Sleepy Hollow*, the route passes the grounds of Leighton Hall Ⓖ (£) and the adjoining village of Yealand Conyers.

PUBS & PIT STOPS

REFRESHMENT ROOMS, Carnforth Station LA5 9TR (01524 732432) Lovingly restored to its 1940s condition as seen in the film.

GIBRALTAR FARM, Silverdale LA5 0UA (01524 701736) Coastal camping near Jenny Brown's Point. Good facilities, reasonable prices. Raw milk from the farm.

THE OLD BAKEHOUSE, Arnside LA5 0HA (01524 761313) Café and takeaway, a good stop for a snack while waiting for the train.

An abundance of choice in Cartmel: At the very top end is **L'ENCLUME** (LA11 6PZ, 015395 36362) and its offshoots; the **PIG & WHISTLE** is the pick of the pubs (LA11 6PL, 015395 36482) and for picnic fixings and damn fine coffee head to the shops at Unsworth's Yard (LA11 6QD).

MASONS ARMS, Strawberry Bank, Cartmel Fell LA11 6NW (015395 68486) Outstanding country inn with rooms and top-notch food.

HARE & HOUNDS, Bowland Bridge LA11 6NN (015395 68038) Stylish 17th-century coaching inn with restaurant and plush bedrooms.

MOSS HOWE FARM CAMPSITE, Witherslack LA11 6SA (015395 52585) Peaceful, well-equipped campsite and yurts in the wonderful Witherslack Valley. Fires allowed.

WITHERSLACK COMMUNITY SHOP, Witherslack LA11 6RH (015395 52188) Home-made cakes and groceries from this bike-friendly shop.

HARE & HOUNDS, Levens LA8 8PN (015395 60004) Much-modernised old coaching inn, food served all day. Rooms.

BIKE SHOP: Dyno-Start, Carnforth. LA5 9JY (01524 732089) Family-run bike shop with a cycle museum upstairs. Vanilla Bikes, Carnforth LA5 9BX (01524 734300).

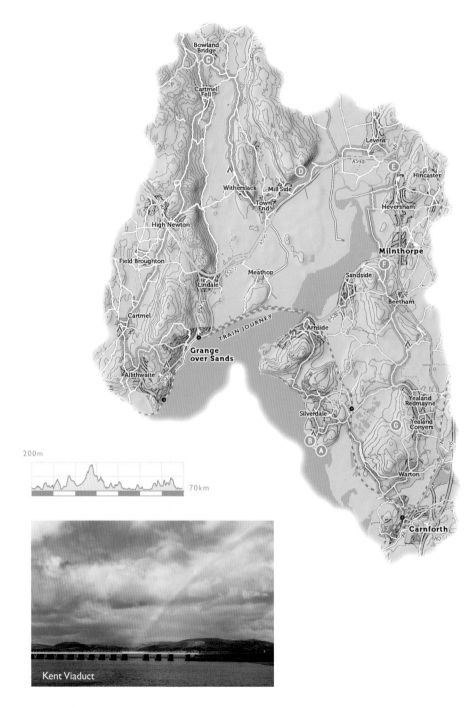

Bowland
Bridge
Ⓒ

Cartmel
Fell

A590

Levens

Ⓔ

Hincaster

Witherslack   Mill Side
Ⓓ

Heversham

Town
End

High Newton

Milnthorpe
Ⓕ

Field Broughton

Sandside

Meathop

Beetham

Lindale

Cartmel

Arnside

TRAIN JOURNEY

Grange
over Sands

Yealand
Redmayne

Allithwaite

Silverdale

Yealand
Conyers

Ⓖ

Ⓑ
Ⓐ

Warton

200m

70km

Carnforth

Kent Viaduct

Jenny Brown's Point

ORGANISED
RIDES

No. 31

DON'T KEEP TO THE ROAD

A fun and friendly audax ride taking in some of the best
gravel tracks of the North York Moors

———

The North York Moors has some of the best gravel riding in Northern England thanks to the network of tracks along the route of the Victorian tramways built for the dozens of mines and quarries that once dotted the moors. The main industry was iron, but there was also alum and coal; the moors are the only source of jet in the Britain.

The ride takes its name from the 1981 cult classic horror comedy film *An American Werewolf in London*. The action begins with a pair of young American backpackers on the North York Moors. After a famously uncomfortable encounter with hostile locals at the Slaughtered Lamb pub, they are warned to keep to the road, stay off the moors and beware the full moon. It's advice they fail to heed and it all gets very grisly very quickly.

The ride is organised by Dean Clementson, an accomplished long-distance cyclist and a leading light in VeloClub 167, the premier audax cycling club of the north east. What Dean doesn't know about the country lanes, tracks and byways of his patch of the North is not worth knowing. He draws on this encyclopaedic knowledge to put on four events which range from a gentle, local 50km to a titanic 300km ride to Cumbria and back. In between, in terms of distance, are Dean's two favourite routes, a 100km and a 150km, which he describes as "hilly, semi off-road circuits of the North York Moors with evil hills, off-road climbs and descents, abandoned railways, hidden valleys, forestry trails and pubs". For me, the 100km was just right, with enough

time to stop and look around, take a midway lunch stop at the famous Lion Inn (far friendlier than the Slaughtered Lamb) and another at the surprise spread of tea and cakes out of a motorhome in one of the wooded dales beneath the high moor. As a late-April event, the weather is always a risk, but the reward is the full range of late spring flora, particularly bluebells which shimmer in iridescent swathes around Cockayne. A few of the climbs are too steep or too rough to ride, but that's just part of the fun of going off-road.

The event HQ is on a farm in the Vale of Mowbray on the western side of the moors between Thirsk and Northallerton. The host is Mike Metcalfe, another serious mile-eater (Mike was the first to 'Everest' Rosedale Chimney and Boltby Bank, two of the most fearsome climbs in the moors). Camping is an option and the whole event has a friendly, festive feel, from the keg of beer, to the sound system, to the home-made cakes Dean pedals over on his cargo bike from Darlington.

Another grassroots event, the MoorsOn-eHundred, a weekend of bikepacking, camping and exploring, is based out of the excellent High Paradise Farm and usually takes place towards the end of May.

Start/finish: Newby Wiske, near Thirsk.
Usually held on a Saturday in April. Camping available at the event HQ for a charity donation.
£5
aukweb.net

VELO RETRO

A well-dressed weekend of vintage bikes and more in the South Lakes

———

Modern factory-made carbon and aluminium bikes might be faster and lighter with better and more reliable gears and brakes, but for looks nothing beats a classic hand-built steel frame complete with polished silver wheel and components that sparkle like diamonds in the sunshine. A vintage bike is an essential item at Velo Retro, the only retro cycling event in the Lake District. It's based out of Ulverston, a small market town on the Furness Peninsula, which makes for a great base for heading north to the Lakes or exploring the West Cumbrian coast. The town itself is much less touristy than the Lake District honeypots of Keswick and Windermere, its narrow, cobbled streets filled with small independent shops.

First run in 2014, it's organised by Alan and Alison Brenton, who took their inspiration from L'Eroica, the original vintage bike ride held each year in Tuscany. It went so well that it inspired a whole Retro Rendezvous weekend that encompasses music, dance, food, markets, classic cars, motorcycles, film and more. There are three rides to suit most appetites, but the 50-mile L'Ancienne is probably the one to go for. It heads north along the flank of the Coniston Old Man before rounding Coniston Water and climbing to Tarn Hows before heading back south along the Windermere cycle path, looping back via Esthwaite Water and Grizedale. A last hurrah is an optional final climb up a track to the John Barrow monument, by special permission of the landowners.

"Most of our money goes on food," confesses organiser Alan. There are two refreshment stops. The first is overlooking Coniston Water where sandwiches and cream teas are served. The second is in a village hall and run by a local WI group who fully embrace the 1950s vibe. "They lay out some massive cakes," says Alan. "It's great to see people's faces when they arrive." The event is limited to no more than 300 riders and there are no big sponsors to distract from the relaxed and friendly atmosphere.

As for bikes, the rule of thumb is that pre-1987 machines are best, with non-aero brakes and no clip-in pedals. But Alan takes a relaxed view of things. "What we care about is that you look the part. We have had the odd person turn up on a modern bike but they are a bit embarrassed and regret they didn't try a bit harder. Everyone knows someone who has an old bike they can borrow for the weekend." There is a prize for the best-turned-out rider and bike, and there have been some stunners, from a British racing green bike with a child's sidecar, rider and passenger dressed in full tweed, to a completely original French mixte frame bike from 1939.

As well as the marshalled and signposted rides there is a do-it-yourself route, the Mighty Corinthian, which must be one of the toughest cycling challenges in the Lakes. It's a full 300km with 4,000m of climbing, so definitely only for the hardiest of riders. It's free to enter, and the organisers provide a map, route card and guide to riding the route, together with GPX track and certificate of recognition for those who finish.

Start/finish: Ulverston
Usually the middle weekend in July. Event camping available for £12/head.
£30 to £44 depending on event distance
sportivelakes.co.uk/velo-retro

YORK RALLY

The venerable annual gathering of cyclists of all stripes just keeps on rolling

———

Back in Britain's golden age of cycling from the late-1940s to the mid-1960s, the York Rally was the biggest gathering of cyclists in the country, if not the world. Run by the Cyclists' Touring Club (CTC), the weekend featured all kinds of racing, a trade show, talks and exhibitions, rides in the countryside, and a parade through the city to a Sunday service in York Minster. There were prizes for the best-turned-out cycling family, the longest ride to the rally and the best cycle-touring photographs.

It was a grass roots affair but there was star quality in abundance, with the likes of the legendary Yorkshire cyclist Beryl Burton mingling with the crowds, and all the top cycling manufacturers showing off their latest wares. At its peak, well over 20,000 people attended and the grassy expanse of the Knavesmire became a temporary tent city. The rally continued through the 1970s and 80s but numbers slowly dwindled. In 2012 the CTC withdrew its support for the event. After a couple of fallow years, a determined group of volunteers revived the rally in 2015 and it's grown every year, though still a far cry from the heyday.

The weekend still features camping on the Knavesmire (with plentiful hot showers available), grass track racing, cyclocross, around a dozen rides for all abilities and all distances, including family-friendly rides along the pan-flat and traffic-free Solar System cycle route, a vintage bike ride and a 100km audax. York is blessed with an abundance of brilliant pubs and a Friday evening pub crawl ride takes in a few of them. There's another evening countryside night ride stopping for fish and chips along the way. In the trade and bike jumble area there are bargains to be had from specialist Spa Cycles as well as a Sunday morning bike jumble and auction of second-hand bikes.

The continuity with the old York Rally is clear – there are hundreds of veteran clubmen and women, some lovely steel bicycles and more tandems, trikes and recumbents than most other bike gatherings. In all its diversity, the one constant is love of cycling. But the future of the rally is by no means certain. A couple of rainy years could spell disaster, and, however hard the volunteer organisers work to put on the event, its success depends on the support and participation of the people who come along. The York Rally is a cycling tradition worth cherishing.

Held at the Knavesmire in York
Usually held in mid-June
Free entry, onsite camping from £17 per pitch for the weekend
yorkrally.org

DIRTY REIVER

A challenging weekend of mud, sweat and gears on
the forest trails of Northumberland

"I've got a gravel bike and I'm gonna use it" would work well as the strapline for Dirty Reiver, an event that seeks to address the problem with gravel bikes in a country without a whole lot of gravel. Gravel bikes are, in essence, lightweight drop handlebar road bikes with bigger tyres, lower gears and frame geometry for comfortable all-day riding. They were developed in the United States which has tens of thousands of miles of hard-packed gravel forest tracks, fire roads and unsurfaced rural backroads, and now has a well-established pro-level gravel racing scene.

Britain's off-road tracks, by contrast, tend to be rougher, rockier and muddier, and no gravel racing scene has developed here. That doesn't mean gravel bikes aren't great all-rounders for British conditions. They excel on our country lanes and byways as well as farm tracks, canal towpaths and rural byways. However, one area where US-style gravel tracks abound is deep inside Northumberland's interior. There are many miles of unsurfaced roads built to service the huge swathes of commercial forestry that blanket the English-Scottish borderlands, once home to the lawless border reivers or raiders.

Dirty Reiver is a timed but non-competitive event. Many people do try to get around as fast as they can but the character of the event is more rally than race. It's based at Kielder Castle and there are three distances: 200km, 130km and 65km. There's also an event for electric assist bikes. For the two longer distances there are time cut-offs and any really slow riders will be directed onto shorter courses. There are feed stations with mechanical support, but riders are expected to be self-sufficient and carry basic tools, spares, food and water.

Cycling's rule of thumb is that off-road miles count double, and there's a fair amount of climbing to factor in. The riding is challenging and most people are just happy to finish. The event is best suited to gravel bikes but a cross bike with large 38-40mm tyres or a hardtail MTB can be used. There's camping onsite and food and drink available throughout the weekend. Besides the riding there's a gravel expo at the event village where the leading gravel bike brands are on hand to show off their wares. As an annual coming together of a small but enthusiastic tribe, it's a friendly affair with the emphasis on common endeavour and having a great time on some of the best traffic-free trails in the country.

Start/finish: Kielder Castle
Usually held mid-April
£30 to £45 depending on distance. Sells out fast.
dirtyreiver.co.uk

BOWLAND FOREST POPULAIRE

A long-running entry-level audax on quiet lanes with a festive atmosphere

———

In the late-19th century bicycles were expensive, the preserve of those with money and time – but they were also the fastest things on the roads. In Britain, France and Italy, groups of cyclists began organising timed challenges over set distances, usually around 200km (124 miles) in 14 hours, approximately sunrise to sunset. No mean feat on the bicycles and roads of the times. One Italian group took the name Audax Italiano, from the Latin audax for 'daring' or 'audacious'. In France, Henri Desgrange, founder of the Tour de France, borrowed their name and codified a set of rules.

Audax combines elements of touring and racing into something quite unlike either. An audax (randonnée or brevet are other names) is a group ride on a set route, with a time limit – but it's not a race, and times are not recorded. There is an element of self-sufficiency: with no arrows showing the way, riders navigate from a route sheet with turn-by-turn instructions, checking in at control points on the way to have their brevet cards stamped. It can seem a little daunting to the uninitiated, but it's a friendly world, and new riders are always welcomed. Today there are long and even international rides, but there are also audaxes of much more manageable distances.

At the shorter brevet populaire distance of 100km the Bowland Forest Populaire is a good first taste of audax or just a very nice day out on the bike. It's well attended by local cycle touring clubs and the atmosphere is friendly and in no way competitive. The route varies from year to year, but tends to make a circuit of the Forest of Bowland rather than plunging through the middle on the famous Trough of Bowland. It starts and finishes in the handsome sandstone village of Wray, and is timed to coincide with the annual Scarecrow Festival at the end of April. The village is en fete for a week, with hundreds of scarecrows made by local residents on display. As is usual with an audax, there is no signage on the route, but riders are given a route card and, if required, a GPX file. There are several control points where you get your brevet card stamped, and plenty of places to pick up refreshments along the way. On return to Wray the village hall has a fine spread of lunch, cakes, teas and coffees.

Start/finish: Wray
Usually held on the Sunday in April
£8 (£5 for Cycling UK and Audax UK members)
ctclancaster.org.uk/audax

PANNIER SOLSTICE WEEKENDER

A sociable weekend of cycle camping in the northern Peak District

———

The popular image of cycling is dominated by bicycle racing. All the way back to Ancient Greece, and probably long before that, people have idolised speed, strength and endurance. 'Scorching' has always been more glamorous and exciting than 'pootling'. It is no wonder so many people associate cycling with hard work, sweat and suffering, and conclude that it's not for them.

Pannier has been helping to turn the tide against the speed freaks since 2012. Sheffield-based cyclist Stefan Amato started the company after a relaxed cycle tour with friends riding from Land's End to John o' Groats. His aim was to build a website where people could find out about long-distance cycling routes and buy the best available kit. Pannier has since branched out into organising adventurous cycling holidays in the UK and overseas.

"Wild routes, cooking out, the social side of bikepacking and cycle touring is the main aspect for us," says Stefan. "We're about friendly group riding in wild places."

The Solstice Weekender is a regular landmark in the Pannier calendar. The format is simple: meet at a city centre location in the north of England on a Saturday nearest the summer solstice, and ride out into the hills where the Pannier camp has already been set up. There are teepees, a camp fire, a camp kitchen and basic facilities. It's all very rustic.

Food is all laid on, with not an energy bar in sight. Lunches are a ploughman's affair of bread and cheese, pickled onions, scotch eggs and hot drinks. Saturday evening is a hearty stew around the campfire with plenty of carbs and a good selection of drinks available. There are a few people on hand to give fireside talks about their own bike adventures.

After breakfast on Sunday it's the 'loaded hill climb' competition. "It's our tongue-in-cheek nod to traditional hill climbing," explains Stefan, "but instead of drilling holes in our saddles and not eating for six months we whack a load of stuff on the bikes. It's a minute and a half, all-out effort." On Sunday it's a ride back to the city, following a different route along quiet lanes and choice gravel tracks.

Attendance is limited to 50 people, which keeps things friendly and informal. The gender balance is healthy and there's usually about a half and half split between Pannier regulars and new faces. Everyone rides out together so there's no field full of parked cars, and they bring only what they can carry on their bikes, which makes the weekend a good way to give cycle camping a try before doing it independently. People are free to bed down in one of the teepees or bring a tent of their own. Pannier has bikes and a full range of touring kit available for loan so it's possible to turn up at the start with just the clothes you're standing in. It all adds up to a fun, sociable, inclusive and accessible weekend away.

Start/finish: Usually Sheffield, but check ahead
A weekend close to the summer solstice (21 June)
£89, including camping, meals and all non-alcoholic drinks
pannier.cc

Lost Lanes North
36 Glorious Bike Rides
in Northern England

Words and photos:
Jack Thurston

Cover illustrations:
Andrew Pavitt

Design and layout:
Amy Bolt

Editorial:
Michael Lee

Proofreading:
Jo Mortimer and
ProofProfessor

Distributed by:
Central Books Ltd
1, Heath Park Industrial Estate,
Freshwater Rd,
Dagenham RM8 1RX
Tel +44 (0)845 458 9911
orders@centralbooks.com

Mapping powered by:

Published by:
Wild Things Publishing Ltd
Freshford, Bath, BA2 7WG
hello@wildthingspublishing.com
www.wildthingspublishing.com

lostlanes.co.uk
Twitter @jackthurston
Instagram: @_lostlanes
#lostlanes
#lostlanesnorth

256

Photographs and maps

All photographs © Jack Thurston except p.35 (top and middle) © Daniel Start, p.101 (bottom left) © Colin Gregory / CC-BY, p.156 © Rab Lawrence / CC-BY, p.164 (right) © Rob Glover / CC-BY, p.241 (top left) © ARG_Flickr / CC-BY, p.242-3 and p.246 © Steve Fleming, p.250 © Andrew Heading, p.254 (top) © Mat Waudby/pannier.cc, p.254 (bottom) © Dave Sear/pannier.cc. Map data © OpenStreetMap, licensed under the Open Database Licence. Additional data from Ordnance Survey, licensed under the Open Government Licence (© Crown copyright and database right 2018).

Acknowledgements

I'm grateful to everyone who has joined me on research trips, modelled for photographs and ridden up 'just one more hill'. Thanks to Harry Adès, Matthew Walters, Adam and Annie Hayes, Tim Carter, Mark Hudson, Des Riley, Ben Brown, Will Linford, Brant Richards, and Dave, Fiona and Ellie Jones. Thank you to all those who gave me tips and ideas, checked routes or otherwise helped, including Harriet McDougal, Rob Ainsley, Ian Williams, Jack Taylor, Stefan Amato, Dean Clementson, Julian Hodgson, Gavin Renshaw, Dave Flitcroft, John Baker, Andy Williamson, Alan Brenton and Graeme Holdsworth. Sorry I couldn't fit everything in.

Massive thanks to Andrew Pavitt for a stunner of a cover and to Amy Bolt for the impeccable design work, especially the maps for which my thanks also go to Richard Fairhurst at cycle.travel. Thank you to Michael Lee for shepherding me through the writing process and keeping me honest and (I hope) interesting. The responsibility for any mistakes is all mine. Thank you, Daniel and Tania, for believing in Lost Lanes and bringing a new book to fruition with all the dedication, encouragement and support I could ask for. Finally, my love and heartfelt thanks to Sarah, Lewin and Rosa for making family life on two wheels so much fun and for not missing me too much when I've been away on the road.

Other books from Wild Things Publishing